ENCOUNTERING GOD
Into the Master's Hands

Elsie Ola

Devotional & Prayers

ENCOUNTERING GOD
Into the Master's Hands
ISBN 978-0-9573406-1-9
© Elsie Ola 2018

All rights reserved

Designed and published in the United Kingdom by HCL Media

A revised and expanded version of Into the Master's Hands (Journal of a Christian, published in 2008)

Unless otherwise indicated, scriptures from the New King James Version (NKJV)
Scriptures marked NKJV are taken from the NEW KING JAMES VERSION (NKJV): Scripture taken from the NEW KING JAMES VERSION®. Copyright© 1982 by Thomas Nelson, Inc. Used by permission. All rights reserved.

Other Scriptures:
Scriptures marked NIV are taken from the NEW INTERNATIONAL VERSION (NIV): Scripture taken from THE HOLY Bible, NEW INTERNATIONAL VERSION ®. Copyright© 1973, 1978, 1984, 2011 by Biblica, Inc.TM. Used by permission of Zondervan
The Jerusalem Bible. Copyright © 1966 by Darton, Longman & Todd Ltd and Doubleday & Company, Inc.
Scriptures marked NLT are taken from the HOLY Bible, NEW LIVING TRANSLATION (NLT): Scriptures taken from the HOLY Bible, NEW LIVING TRANSLATION, Copyright© 1996, 2004, 2007 by Tyndale House Foundation. Used by permission of Tyndale House Publishers, Inc., Carol Stream, Illinois 60188. All rights reserved. Used by permission.
Scriptures marked AMP are taken from the AMPLIFIED Bible (AMP): Scripture taken from the AMPLIFIED® Bible, Copyright © 1954, 1958, 1962, 1964, 1965, 1987 by the Lockman Foundation Used by Permission. (www.Lockman.org)

"Unless the LORD builds the house, they labor in vain who build it; unless the LORD guards the city, the watchman stays awake in vain."
(Psalm 127:1)

"Take delight in the Lord, and he will give you your heart's desires. Commit everything you do to the Lord. Trust him, and he will help you."
(Psalm 37:4-5 NLT)

CONTENTS

	Dedication	7
	Author's Note	9
1	The Father's Heart	13
2	Jesus Lover Of My Soul	16
3	Pleasing Him	19
4	Nuggets From 1 Samuel 1	21
5	Lessons From Numbers Chapters 13 & 14	24
6	Believe It!	26
7	Change Me, O Lord!	29
8	Trusting Him	31
9	It Can Still Happen	35
10	He's Right Here	37
11	Fix My Eyes On Him	39
12	Moving On To Greater Things	41
13	Which Way Please?	43
14	Perilous Times	46
15	Do Something With Your Faith	49
16	His Word At Work In Me	51
17	I Have A Testimony	53
18	Determined To Succeed	55
19	Live For Him	57
20	To Be Childlike Again	59
21	Being Thankful	61
22	I Have Done It Again!	64
23	He That Is In Me	66
24	For God's Sake	68
25	I Can Wake Up To Change	71
26	A God Of Purpose	73
27	No One Can Reverse His Works	76
28	Don't Be Someone Else	79
29	Going All The Way	83

30	His Vessel	86
31	How Do You See Him?	88
32	He Is Working On Us	90
33	Rest In Him	93
34	Be a Blessing	95
35	Hands Off!	97
36	He's Not Partial	100
37	Good Enough For God?	102
38	He Knows How To Speak	105
39	God's Work In Progress	107
40	You've Been Set Free	110
41	Don't Despise What You Have	112
42	You Don't Love Me	115
43	My Own Strength	117
44	Don't Lose Heart	120
45	God's Creation	123
46	God Has a Plan	126
47	God Has His Ways	129
48	Precepts Of Life From Hebrews 12	131
49	The Power Of Prayer	135
50	Prayers	145

- Prayers seeking after God (145)
- Praying for a transformed life (146)
- Praying to break hindrances (148)
- Praying for protection (150)
- Praying for a miracle (151)
- Prayers for ministry (152)
- Praying for the month (153)
- Praying for your spouse (155)
- Praying for the nation and others (156)
- Praying in pursuit of purpose (158)
- Praying against the works of the enemy (160)
- Praying against witchcraft (161)
- Praying for wholeness (162)

DEDICATION

To God Most High who preserves me and has called me through Jesus Christ to be a light for Him — love, hugs and kisses. Thank You Lord. I pray that this book will cause every one who reads it to encounter Your Presence like they have never before.

I also have to make mention of my darling husband Wale and the wonderful children God has blessed us with, Jordan, Jesse and Joella — I love you lots.

AUTHOR'S NOTES

The original book, Into the Master's Hand (Journal of a Christian) published in 2008 through Xulon Press was birthed from daily journals that I started keeping from 2004. I picked up the book to read five years later and as I read, I suddenly got the inspiration to revise and expand it. I started doing so, but I was unable to complete till now. I believe this is God's perfect timing, because in the years between, He has been working on me and we have also changed our family name from Oladimeji to Ola. As I said previously in the first book, God gave me the title "Into the Master's Hand" as I was waking from sleep and when the time was ripe, He inspired me to put the notes together.

As I picked up my notes to continue to put this book together "Encountering God Devotional" dropped in my heart. My heart's desire and prayer is that your relationship with the Lord will be greatly enhanced as you read and pray along. May you encounter God in a profound, life changing way and may the eyes of your understanding be opened to comprehend His love for you and His will for your life.

If you have never at any time invited Jesus Christ into your heart to be your Lord and Saviour, please reach out to Him today. He is calling out to you and wants to shower you with His goodness and mercy. The scripture says in Romans 10:9-11 *"that if you confess with your mouth the Lord Jesus and believe in your heart that God has raised Him from the dead, you will be saved. For with the heart one believes unto righteousness, and with the mouth confession is made unto salvation. For the Scripture says, "Whoever believes on Him will not be put to shame."*

Pray this prayer: *"Dear Lord Jesus, please forgive me my sins and cleanse me from all unrighteousness. I repent of my sins and renounce them all. I believe that You are the Son of God, that You died and were raised again from the dead to set me free. I invite You into my heart and into my life to be my Lord and my Saviour. I believe that by faith I am now saved, I am born again. According to Your word I am a new creation and any claim of Satan over my life has been broken by Your sacrifice on the Cross. I receive Your Holy Spirit into my heart right now and I believe that old things have passed away and all things have become new for me today — Amen!"*

If you just said this prayer, I pray that you will be blessed and grow in the knowledge of our God and our Lord Jesus Christ. Three sure ways of doing this is by 1. Finding a Bible-believing, Spirit-filled Church to go to and also telling as many people as you can about your new life. 2. Praying: prayer is simply talking with God and expecting Him to talk to you too. You can talk to Him about anything. You can start by thanking Him for who He is and for what He has done. 3. Reading the Bible. A good place to start is the book of John, then read through the New Testament and then back to Matthew, Mark and Luke. There are various Bible reading plans available out there that are quite helpful. Before you read the Bible or pray, it's always good to ask the Holy Spirit for help so you can understand what you are reading and to inspire your prayers.

1

THE FATHER'S HEART

"For God so loved the world that he gave his one and only Son, that whoever believes in him shall not perish but have eternal life. The Father loves the Son and has placed everything in his hands. Whoever believes in the Son has eternal life, but whoever rejects the Son will not see life, for God's wrath remains on them."
(John 3:16, 35-36 NIV)

What a wonderful Father we have in God. He did not leave us without hope in this world, He did not send an angel to redeem us, He sent His very best, His only begotten Son (Jesus Christ). He did not do this because we were righteous or good, but while we were still deep in sin, Christ died for us. Even while He was going through all the torment and torture just for us, man was still rejecting Him and shouting *"Crucify Him! Crucify Him!"*, yet He did not back down nor did He call forth the angels to destroy them, instead He said *"Father, forgive them, for they do not know what they do"* (Mark 15:13; Luke 23:34). What depth of love this is, that He still bothers with man even when we still deny Him in our daily lives. He still woos us with His love and mercy.

This love is typified in the story of the prodigal son and the father that Jesus spoke of in Luke 15:11-32. We see in the story how the younger son took his inheritance from his father and left home to go live a life of so called "merriment". You know how it is when people think that the grass is greener on the other side, till they find out that it's just deception. He soon came to his senses when life dealt him blow after blow, he realised that he had a home to go to. He was even prepared to be like one of the servants, but the father seeing him coming from afar off, ran to meet him with open arms.

God our Father is love and is reaching out to you so that He can embrace you with His love. He has a good plan for your life and wants to mould you into a vessel of honour. He wants to pour His love into you and use you to demonstrate His love to those that do not know Him, because they have not received Him through His only begotten Son, Jesus Christ, who is the One that has qualified us to be adopted by the Father. 1 John 2:23 says, *"Whoever denies the Son does not have the Father either; he who acknowledges the Son has the Father also."*

He loves with such a pure love that He disciplines us when He needs to for our own good, so that we are not destroyed. Whenever we hurt He feels it, whenever we are weak, He wants us to call on Him for strength; when we are troubled He so wants to help us. If only we can understand the depth of love that He has for us, then we will live for Him.

PRAY:

Father help me to know You more and let my life show forth

Your glory.

Let me abide in Your love and let Your love radiate through me, so that all can see that I am Yours and You are mine.

1 John 3
Psalm 91

2

JESUS, THE LOVER OF MY SOUL

"But God showed his great love for us by sending Christ to die for us while we were still sinners."
(Romans 5:8 NLT)

I cannot imagine life without Him. A life without hope, a life without real purpose — a life whose path leads to destruction. I am glad I found Him or should I say, I am glad He let me find Him. I am amazed at the depth of love He has for me. Me...? Yes, He loves me regardless of where I've been or what I've done. Why does He love me? I do not know, but He does! He loved me even when I seemed unlovable. He loved me even when I was deep in sin. He loved me even though I did not really know Him.

He took me and cleansed me with His love and made me into a precious jewel in His hands. Still I stumble and He loves me nevertheless. This knowledge truly amazes me. Why does He bother? If He chooses not to love me, what can I do to Him? I'm so glad that loving me is not an option for Him — it is who He is. What an honour, what a privilege to be called His very own.

It is a shame to live in this world without truly knowing

who He really is. When we fix all our hopes and cares on the things of this world, we are to be greatly pitied. When what we rely on is the love of a man or the love of a woman, then what great misery awaits us if that love fails. The love of man may grow cold, but the love of God remains constant, in the good and in the bad times He remains the same. In Psalm 27:10 the psalmist says, *"When my father and my mother forsake me, then the LORD will take care of me."*

His love gives our souls the peace and the joy that is needed so that life here on earth is not a chore. His love fills that God-shaped hole in our hearts, the God-shaped hole that is in the heart of every man that can only be filled by Him. In Acts 17:16-33, we see where Paul tells the men gathered around him about Jesus Christ and the way that God wants to be worshipped. He tells them that God has made us humans that we may seek Him, because it's in Him that we live, we move and have our being. Isn't this truly amazing that the Creator of the heavens and the earth and everything seen and unseen would love us so much

PRAY:

Thank You so much Lord Jesus for giving Yourself as a ransom for my soul. Lord truly be the centre of my life. Let my affection for You not be in words only but in spirit and in truth. Be the most important person in my life — let this be reflected in everything that I do and everything that I say.

Be found in me my Lord. Manifest through me, so that everyone that meets me encounter You, that they may come to

know and adore You, the one and only true God .

John 3:1-21
John 14:19-24

3

PLEASING HIM

"Let the words of my mouth and the meditation of my heart be acceptable in Your sight, O LORD, my strength and my Redeemer." (Psalm 19:14)

This is my prayer indeed. With all the different types of people and situations that one has to deal with, I truly need God's grace and strength not to think, wish or say evil about anyone. I pray that my ways may please the Lord, knowing that if I have favour with Him, then He is able to give me favour with people. I know that I can't buy His love with good deeds, because He loves me anyway, however, He says in the book of John 14:15 *"If you love Me, keep My commandments."* And John 15:9-10 *"As the Father loved Me, I also have loved you; abide in My love. If you keep My commandments, you will abide in My love, just as I have kept My Father's commandments and abide in His love."* So if I say I am His, then I want to live my life in a manner that pleases Him, in obedience to His word.

I've come to realise that you cannot please everyone; the harder you try at times the more you may be misunderstood. I simply just ask God to give me the grace to love regardless because this is what He requires of me. I hold on to His word in Proverbs 16:7 "When a man's ways please the Lord, He makes even his enemies to be at peace with him."

I have also come to realise that I'm not perfect (surprise, surprise!), but I really want to be, because He is. Thank God that even with all my weaknesses He still loves me and His hand is still upon me, so who am I to hold a grudge against another. As hard as this is, I choose not to for my own sake, and I know that He will help me.

PRAY:

Lord help me to live my life in a manner that is acceptable to You. Grant me the grace to love the things that You love and to hate the things that You hate.

Help me to be patient and to see people through the eyes of love, making excuses for them (if possible) knowing that they may be dealing with issues in their lives that have tainted their perception and their personality.

1 Thessalonians 4:1-12
Hebrews 12

4

NUGGETS FROM 1 SAMUEL 1

"Trust in Him at all times, you people; pour out your heart before Him; God is a refuge for us."
(Psalm 62:8)

There are times that you may appear blessed, but in certain areas of your life you are barren — maybe not physical barrenness, but emotional, financial or spiritual barrenness. You may see people around you flourishing in your area of lack or barrenness, however in your life there is no fruit; and it's been like this for years and it looks like time is running out. People may criticise you, they may talk about you, and they may not give you the honour that is due to you. Same thing happened to Hannah; her husband, Elkanah's other wife used to make fun of her predicament. This went on for several years, till it got too much for her.

What did she do? One day on one of the family's annual trip to Shiloh to worship and sacrifice to the LORD of Hosts, She went into the tabernacle and prayed fervently like a drunken woman. Though her lips were moving you could not hear her words because they were welling up from deep within her (like groans). I believe that she reached the point where she was tired of the situation and had to pour out her heart before the Lord. She knew that pouring out her heart before men would not help the situation — she had to go to her God "one on one". God used Eli the Priest to pronounce a blessing on her (*1 Samuel 1:17*), and she received it (*1 Samuel 1:18*).

Make sure you get a word from God to hold on to and run with. Whatever the case, don't fret but trust God, He sees the bigger picture. Take your petitions to Him, desperate cases call for fervent prayers. Hannah made a vow to the Lord that if He would remember her and give her a son, she would give him back to the Lord. I believe you need to get to the place where you are willing to lay your desires down at the feet of Jesus before or even after they have been fulfilled. When He does cause you to give birth to something great, you must realise that whatever you birth belongs to Him and therefore should not be a reason to boast.

Hannah honoured her vow to the Lord, by taking the child to the House of God and leaving him there after she had weaned him. Imagine something she had desperately longed for, not a daughter, but a son (as this was dear to them in those days), a son that she could take all around town to show off with. Obviously she was at peace with God, and the fact that He had opened her womb was sufficient for her. She could smile at her enemies because she rejoiced in the salvation of the Lord. Merciful God gave her more sons and daughters as a reward for her obedience.

What is the conclusion of this matter? Do not let your problems consume you or drive you away from God, but rather let them drive you into His Presence, where there is fullness of joy. May the Lord take away your reproach and cause your mouth to be full of thanksgiving and praise as you rejoice in His salvation. The Lord once said to me "In the wilderness build an altar unto the Lord". Likewise I say to you, while you are waiting for the promise or the divine intervention of the Lord, build an altar of thanksgiving, praise and worship unto Him.

PRAY:

Lord come to my rescue and breathe into every area of my life, so that I may bear fruits that will prosper me and bring glory to You.

Answer me Lord as I call to You. (Now bring your request before Him.)

1 Samuel 1
Daniel 3:8-30

5

LESSONS FROM NUMBERS CHAPTERS 13 & 14

"The steps of a good man are ordered by the LORD, And He delights in his way."
(Psalm 37:23)

- God made them a promise.
- They saw the land and the giants in it (the natural circumstances that seemed impossible to conquer).
- They looked at their own natural abilities rather than look to the Creator, the supernatural God with whom nothing is impossible.
- Caleb saw right! I am sure he remembered the faithfulness of God: how He delivered them in times past. He parted the Red Sea for them to walk through on dry ground, He gave them manna to eat and quail for meat; all the signs and wonders He worked in Egypt to deliver them from oppression and bondage. Caleb possibly thought to himself, "If God could do all that, then this is a small thing for Him to do."
- The people grumbled and complained as we often do, rather than seek God in prayer — for strength, strategy, wisdom, grace, or whatever was needed for the task ahead.

- Thank God for people of good report (Joshua and Caleb) — They knew that it was not going to be by their strength or scheming, but if God said it, He is more than able to bring it to pass. They said, *"If the LORD delights in us, then He will bring us into this land and give it to us..."* (Numbers 14:8)

So what are you saying about God or the word of God? Be careful who you listen to when God gives you a promise whether through a prophetic word or His promises to you in the scriptures — whose report would you believe? Are you a believer or a doubter? Are you a grumbler, a complainer or one who appreciates who God is and who takes Him at His word? Let us imitate those who through faith and patience inherit the promise (Hebrews 6:12). *"He who calls you is faithful, who also will do it."* (I Thessalonians 5:24)

PRAY:

Lord grant me the grace to look beyond the natural circumstances around me. Teach me how to delight myself in You and to walk with You day by day.

Lord give me the strategies that I need to conquer every giant in my life.

Judges 7
2 Chronicles 20

6

BELIEVE IT!

"The nobleman said to Him, "Sir, come down before my child dies!" Jesus said to him, "Go your way; your son lives." So the man believed the word that Jesus spoke to him, and he went his way. And as he was now going down, his servants met him and told him, saying, "Your son lives!""
(John 4:49-51)

There are times that God reveals great things to us, whether in a vision, a dream, by prophecy or in the Bible that we struggle to believe. Just like the men who went to spy out the promised land with Joshua and Caleb. These promises sometimes seem rather daunting or far-fetched, and maybe like Sarah in Genesis 18:13-15 you may even laugh, thinking how can this thing be? Well, He is the Most High God, is there anything too difficult for Him to accomplish?

I use my own situation as an example: when God spoke great words into my life on my fortieth birthday, I began to struggle to pray, to study the Bible and even to wait on the Lord. I almost began to wonder how these things will be seeing that I'm struggling to push through, but after reading the above verses from John Chapter four again, it encouraged me to simply believe what He has told me. Even in my struggles I must fix my eyes on Him and surely He will bring it to pass.

I decided that I must consciously and continually thank Him for what He has promised and begin to confess it and do whatever He leads me to do till I see the fullness of the manifestation of all that He has said. Over a decade has gone by and I have begun to walk in part of the promise and still eagerly await the rest. I have found out in this period of waiting for the manifestation of the full promise not to give up, but to do the good that I can do today. I've also found that even when I've been too weak to pray as I ought, I still get on my knees and ask the Holy Spirit to help me, and even if all that comes out of me are like groans, I'm fine with this because according to the word of God, *"Likewise the Spirit also helps in our weaknesses. For we do not know what we should pray for as we ought, but the Spirit Himself makes intercession for us with groanings which cannot be uttered. Now He who searches the hearts knows what the mind of the Spirit is, because He makes intercession for the saints according to the will of God"* (Romans 8:26-27).

The following two scriptures have also greatly influenced and encouraged me in this walk of faith: *"For indeed the gospel was preached to us as well as to them; but the word which they heard did not profit them, not being mixed with faith in those who heard it"* (Hebrews 4:2); and *"Blessed is she who believed, for there will be a fulfilment of those things which were told her from the Lord.* (Luke 1:45). Hold on, your breakthrough is coming!

PRAY:

Lord I thank You for everything You have done in my life, I thank You for everything that You are doing and all that You will do. I surrender myself to Your will for my life.

Lord uphold me by Your mighty power and reign in me. Give me divine strategies of what I should be doing right now in preparation for the greater things that are ahead of me.

John 11
Hebrews 11

7

CHANGE ME, O LORD!

"Create in me a clean heart, O God, And renew a steadfast spirit within me."
(Psalm 51:10)

When asking the Lord to change someone else, think of this for a moment, could the person be asking God to change you too? Or could the problem you have with the person be as a result of your wrong perception or your attitude that needs to change? God wants us to first get rid of the log in our own eye so that we can see well. Maybe when the log is removed from your eye, you may come to realise that the speck you saw in the other person's eye was just a reflection of the log that was in yours.

I simply yield to the Lord and ask Him to change me and to make the other party who He wants them to be; and I have found that He has changed me and He is changing me still. The Bible says in Proverbs 16:2, *"All the ways of a man are pure in his own eyes, but the LORD weighs the spirits."* Even the evil man in all his evil, can try to justify his actions. Imagine if we are all right, who then is wrong?

It is a wonderful prayer that the Psalmist prayed in Psalm

19:12-14 and I use this as part of my prayers: Lord, cleanse me from secret faults, keep me back from presumptuous sins, let them not rule over me. Let my thoughts, words and actions please You and help me Lord to see myself as You see me; help me also to change, because I certainly know that there are many things in me that need changing. (Make this your prayer too.)

PRAY:

Have mercy on me O Lord and forgive me my sins. I repent for when I have judged others unjustly.

Lord flood my heart with light and help me see right.

Psalm 51
1 John 2

8

TRUSTING HIM

"You will keep him in perfect peace, Whose mind is stayed on You, Because he trusts in You."
(Isaiah 26:3)

While waking up from a dream one morning, I heard the words "God is trying to teach you not to trust in the arm of flesh." Who? Me? I felt to read Jeremiah 17:5-8 NLT which says, *"This is what the Lord says: "Cursed are those who put their trust in mere humans, who rely on human strength and turn their hearts away from the Lord. They are like stunted shrubs in the desert, with no hope for the future. They will live in the barren wilderness, in an uninhabited salty land. "But blessed are those who trust in the Lord and have made the Lord their hope and confidence. They are like trees planted along a riverbank, with roots that reach deep into the water. Such trees are not bothered by the heat or worried by long months of drought. Their leaves stay green, and they never stop producing fruit."* When our eyes are fixed only on what human strength can accomplish, we tend to forget to look to God as our source. We can get so fixated on our own natural abilities or what other people can do for us that we do not look to God our Maker to help us. We may even ignore Him who alone is all knowing and all wise and toil and toil, many times to no avail, or compromise to attain much with plenty sorrow at times, whereas we have a God who can help us. Many times we take our focus off Him and put it on other people, while He takes a backseat in our hearts or our hearts may even depart from Him. Imagine putting your trust in a person who is not able to keep himself or herself alive, neither is he or she able to determine what their tomorrow will be. What if you offend them? What happens then? There is also a likelihood to overlook whatever evil those we are looking to as our source are doing, because we don't want to offend them, lest they withhold help from us.

For some, it's not really trusting in your own abilities as such because you don't feel you have any. We can fret and cry because it seems like we have little strength and no abilities and don't know what to do. We feel bereft of ideas. We look everywhere for answers and help rather than go to God for direction, wisdom and divine empowerment, so we end up being miserable and defeated.

Another way in which we can make the arm of flesh (people) our strength is when someone close to you always compliments you, it makes you feel good and there is a tendency that you may begin to get your validation from such a person, especially when others may think otherwise. This is dangerous because one's validation (the one that matters) should be from God and from Him alone. If we please God it doesn't matter if we displease man, because He is able to cause even our enemies to be at peace with us if necessary (Proverbs 16:7), but if we displease God, does it matter who we please? The truth is that eventually if you do not say or do the right things to cater to people, their opinion of you may change. So what happens to your validation?

In writing this, I now understand what the Lord is talking about in teaching me not to trust in the arm of flesh. I have had several experiences in the past where people will get to know me and say all sorts of nice things about me and I'll let that be my validation, but at the end of the day when they feel I'm not as close to them as they think I should be or I am not as "understanding" as they think I should be, they become unpleasant. I have since come to realise that low self-esteem at times causes one to seek validation from others, but this is just a set up for disappointment.

My summation is that God called me and not man. As long as He is pleased with me and I have favour with Him, He will give me favour with everyone I need favour from, and use them to accomplish whatever He needs them to accomplish in my life. Even when receiving compliments, I must always remember to give the praise, honour and glory back to God, never forgetting that He and He alone is my strength, my strong tower, my refuge in the day of trouble, the glory and the lifter of my head. I will also not put my trust in what I can accomplish in my own strength or what man can do for me, I will put my trust in the Lord who has made me and His grace that is abundant to me, and lean on Him so that my boast will not be on self but in the power of God. We've got to realise that whatever we have or whatever we can do is because of the grace that He gives us in the first place, therefore all the glory must go to Him.

PRAY:

Lord You are my strength, my refuge, my provider, my protector, my firm foundation; I am nothing apart from You. I put my trust in You.

I yield my heart to You dear Lord, mould me and make me after Your will.

1 Kings 13
Luke 12:13-21

9

IT CAN STILL HAPPEN

"For with God nothing will be impossible."
(Luke 1:37)

Take comfort from this scripture, because at times situations around us or in our lives may look bleak and may seem as though there is no hope, no way out; take heart, for with God all things are possible. Somehow, God is able to turn every situation around and bring good out of all that we go through as we trust Him and allow Him to work His purpose in our lives. What He doesn't make happen for us may be because we do not need it to achieve what He has called us to do.

The Bible tells us that He makes a way in the wilderness and rivers in the desert (Isaiah 43:19). I have many personal testimonies of His goodness in my life that I cannot put on paper. Times when there seemed to be no way, when as a family we had not known where food was coming from and then someone rings the doorbell to deliver groceries. There are so many testimonies of divine intervention that point not only to the greatness, but also to the mercy and goodness of God. Hallelujah!

1 Corinthians 10:13 NLT says *"The temptations in your life are*

no different from what others experience. And God is faithful. He will not allow the temptation to be more than you can stand. When you are tempted, he will show you a way out so that you can endure." My prayer for you is that whatever you are going through in life that you will put your hands in the hands of the Master. Even if you can't see the way out, He knows the way. He will not let you drown. There is hope for you in Him if you would only believe.

PRAY:

Lord surround me with Your peace and help me to live the life of an overcomer.

O Lord God come to my rescue. Be a wall of fire around me and keep me from all evil.

Mark 9:14-29
Daniel 6

10

HE'S RIGHT HERE

"Where can I go from Your Spirit? Or where can I flee from Your presence? If I ascend into heaven, You are there; If I make my bed in hell, behold, You are there. If I take the wings of the morning, And dwell in the uttermost parts of the sea, Even there Your hand shall lead me, And Your right hand shall hold me. If I say, "surely the darkness shall fall on me," even the night shall be light about me; Indeed, the darkness shall not hide from You, but the night shines as the day; The darkness and the light are both alike to You."
(Psalm 139:7-12)

Why have I written this? To encourage myself in the Lord, because I know that wherever I am He is there with me. There are times as we pass through life that we are in places or circumstances where we feel all alone, but we have the assurance that He is there with us, whether we feel Him or not. He is Jehovah Shammah, the LORD who is always there. He has said that He will never leave us nor forsake us (Hebrews 13:5) and if He is for us who can be against us? (Romans 8:31).

He is Light, therefore whatever darkness surrounds me must flee before Him. He lights up my life with His radiance and causes me to shine in the midst of darkness. His hand is forever leading me and carrying me whenever I am weak and feel I can't go on –- His loving kindness and tender mercies never cease to amaze me.

Job during the most trying time in his life said this, *"Look, I go forward, but He is not there, And backward, but I cannot perceive Him; when He works on the left hand, I cannot behold Him; when He turns to the right hand, I cannot see Him. But He knows the way that I take; when He has tested me, I shall come forth as gold."* (Job 23:8-10). Though it seemed to him as though God wasn't there with him in his trials, he was still confident in the fact that even though he could not see God, God knows all things and sees all things and was able to locate him wherever he was at. He refused to curse God, but instead was still going after God.

PRAY:

Lord even though I can't see You, nor feel You, I know that You are with me; and that You are on my case. I rest in You.

Lord let Your loving kindness and Your tender mercies surround me.

Isaiah 43:1-19
Hebrews 4

11

FIX MY EYES ON HIM

"I can do all things through Christ who strengthens me."
(Philippians 4:13)

I just have this confidence that when I call on the Lord and fix my eyes on Him that I am able to do all things, even things that seem impossible or hard for me to do — which are quite a lot of things. This is what keeps me going despite the odds, because He has promised to always be with me. Isaiah 43:2 says, *"When you pass through the waters, I will be with you; and when you pass through the rivers, they will not sweep over you. When you walk through the fire, you will not be burned; the flames will not set you ablaze."*

He is so faithful, so kind, so loving, so merciful, so good, so great, so mighty, and so awesome; there are not enough words to describe Him — and yet in all this, He wants me to know Him as Father. A Father who is always there for me, even when it seems that I am too busy or too tired to spend much time alone with Him; that doesn't stop Him from being "Abba", my Daddy and certainly doesn't stop Him from loving me. It is even in these times that I've learned to truly appreciate the grace of God the more.

PRAY:

Dear Father, please help me to fix my eyes on You.

Let my life bring pleasure to You and cause glory to abound to You through those who look at my life and see Your handwriting all over it.

1 Chronicles 28
Psalm 121

12

MOVING ON TO GREATER THINGS

"Brethren, I do not count myself to have apprehended; but one thing I do, forgetting those things which are behind and reaching forward to those things which are ahead, I press toward the goal for the prize of the upward call of God in Christ Jesus. Therefore let us, as many as are mature, have this mind; and if in anything you think otherwise, God will reveal even this to you."
(Philippians 3:13-16)

Whether good or bad it can become a snare when we are consumed by the past. As the Apostle Paul encourages us in the above scripture, we need to press on if not we will stagnate, maybe even regress. Christ has so much more laid up for us to accomplish. If life has been cruel, it's time to put these things behind you. In some cases though it might be wise to ask why (depending on what the case is though), not why He let these things happen to you; but could there possibly be anything you need to learn? Or could their be any demonic interference that you need to deal with? So that you can press on with the hope of better things ahead of you. If it's been generally good, thank God.

Whatever the case has been, good or bad, there are better things in store for you in Christ Jesus as you use these experiences as stepping stones rather than letting them become stumbling blocks. In Jesus' name you will get there, for His grace is available to you at your point of need. Take courage in the words of the Lord in John 16:33, "*These things I have spoken to you, that in Me you may have peace. In the world you will have tribulation; but be of good cheer, I have overcome the world.*"

May the peace and joy of the Lord garrison your heart as you tarry in His Presence.

PRAY:

Lord help me to let go of everything that is weighing me down, so that I may run the race you have set for me.

Lord open the eyes of my understanding so that I may see whatever hindrances to destiny there might be in my life.

1 Samuel 17
Exodus 3

13

WHICH WAY PLEASE?

"He has made everything beautiful in it's time. Also He has put eternity in their hearts, except that no one can find out the work that God does from beginning to end."
(Ecclesiastes 3:11)

The New Living translation of the Bible I believe better explains it to me. It says: *"God has made everything beautiful for its own time. He has planted eternity in the human heart, but even so, people cannot see the whole scope of God's work from beginning to end."* If only we could see behind the scene and take a peek at what God has in store for us tomorrow. At times God shows us or tells us where He is taking us. However, He does not tell us the process or the route to this destination, many times not even the timing (Ouch!). Don't you just wish at times that whenever you say, "Which way please?" that you will hear an audible voice from the Lord saying, "This is the way."

Not knowing makes us so restless at times and we begin to speculate on what God is doing or what He is not doing or what He intends to do to get us there. The Lord knows us too well. If He tells us the hindrances and obstacles that we must face on the road to the appointed destination, how many of us will embark on the journey? Yet it is this very route, no matter how uncomfortable it is that will shape us for the inheritance. David had to face Goliath to get to the next level (1 Samuel 17). Some of us may even run ahead of God to get there quicker, however if it's not done His way and in His time, it will not stand. Anyway, it will not be a faith walk would it, if we always knew everything? We are certain that even if we do not know, He knows! Furthermore, and more importantly if we are His, His Spirit is in us to lead us if of course we allow Him to.

This is a good time for someone who doesn't know to ask, "But how do I know that He is leading me?" It all comes down to fellowship; getting to know God through prayer and reading the Word (Yes! The Bible and prayer, there are no shortcuts), because the Holy Spirit will never contradict God's word as He leads you. *"For as many as are led by the Spirit of God, these are the sons of God"* (Romans 8:14). This talks of maturity and intimacy, not just a casual relationship with the Lord.

The truth of the matter is that God loves you and that He is not a wicked God, but a good Father. Whatever you go through, remember the words in Jeremiah 29:11-13 (NIV) which says: *"For I know the plans I have for you," declares the LORD, "plans to prosper you and not to harm you, plans to give you hope and a future. Then you will call upon me and come and pray to me, and I will listen to you. You will seek me and find me when you seek me with all your heart."*

So my advice to you on your journey through life is to submit to God and resist the devil and his suggestions and temptations which are designed to take you off track in order to kill, to steal and to destroy you or your destiny (John 10:10). We just need to trust Him and walk with Him day by day, knowing that His desire for us is that we may have a richly fulfilled life even right here on earth.

PRAY:

Lord please give me spiritual wisdom and insight so that I may grow in my knowledge of You (Ephesians 3:17 NLT).

Father please help me to yield to the leading of the Holy Spirit.

Psalm 32
Psalm 37

14

PERILOUS TIMES

"These things I have spoken to you, that in Me you may have peace. In the world you will have tribulation; but be of good cheer, I have overcome the world."
(John 16:33)

So much evil is being perpetrated in the world today; terrorism, child abuse, sexual abuse and perversion, tropical storms, hurricanes, earthquakes... (to name but a few). In all these, while some are grieving, others are celebrating; while others still don't know whether they are coming or going, whether they are sad or happy. All sorts of evil is happening under the sun that is too sickening to mention.

Truly when the Bible says in 2 Timothy 3:1-4, *"But know this, that in the last days perilous times will come: For men will be lovers of themselves, lovers of money, boasters, proud, blasphemers, disobedient to parents, unthankful, unholy, unloving, unforgiving, slanderers, without self-control, brutal, despisers of good, traitors, headstrong, haughty, lovers of pleasure rather than lovers of God,"* These times are way upon us no doubt!

There is so much evil in the world that sin is being called "good" and holiness being portrayed as "bad" or "old fashioned".

If God, (as recorded in Genesis 6:5-6) when He saw that the wickedness and evil of man was continually great on the earth and was sorry that He had made man and was grieved in His heart; imagine how He feels now. At times the things that I see and hear almost overwhelm my heart, but I take strength from the fact that our Lord Jesus Christ is coming back again and more importantly that He is my strong tower, my stronghold in times of trouble, the Author and Finisher of my faith.

Thank God that the Holy Spirit is with us and in us and leads us into all truth, teaching us things to come and steering us in the right path. If Christ has overcome the world, so can we because His Spirit lives in us and will strengthen and enable us to be triumphant. I take comfort in His word that says that He will not allow us to be tempted more than we can handle, but with the temptation, will also make the way of escape that we may be able to bear it *(1 Corinthians 10:13)*. The New Living Translation (NLT) of the Bible says, *"...When you are tempted, he will show you a way out so that you can endure."* This means that we have to be constantly hooked up to Him so that we may hear Him as He speaks to us in diverse ways.

I leave you with these scriptures: *"Be sober, be vigilant; because your adversary the devil walks about like a roaring lion, seeking whom he may devour. Resist him, steadfast in the faith, knowing that the same sufferings are experienced by your brotherhood in the world."* (1 Peter 5:8-9) and *"Watch and pray, lest you enter into temptation."* (Matthew 26:41).

PRAY:

Lord let Your Kingdom come and Your will be done on earth as it is in heaven (Matthew 6:10). Let the nations return to You and let the Church not compromise the truth in Your word.

Heal the sick Lord, save the lost, comfort the broken hearted, frustrate and destroy the works of the enemy, open blind eyes (spiritual and physical), open deaf ears (spiritual and physical), may the whole earth be filled with the awareness of who You are in Jesus' name.

John 10
2 Timothy 3

15

DO SOMETHING WITH YOUR FAITH

"But someone will say, "You have faith, and I have works." Show me your faith without your works, and I will show you my faith by my works. You believe that there is one God. You do well. Even the demons believe—and tremble! But do you want to know, O foolish man, that faith without works is dead?" (James 2:18-20)

For so long many of us Christians have sat on the sidelines. We complain about issues, but don't do much about it except grumble and at best maybe pray about it. Our prayers are very good, however God is requiring more than our prayers. Certainly we must pray first, but having done that we must take the necessary action. For instance if Christians seeing the state of moral decadence in a nation, pray that God will intervene and He does by bringing a candidate that will help bring the needed change, but we all stay at home come election day, what do you suppose would happen?

If we all stayed at home or in our churches and prayed for souls to be saved and no one goes out to actually evangelise, how will they be saved. In Romans 10:14 the Scripture says, *"How then shall they call on Him in whom they have not believed? And how shall they believe in Him of whom they have not heard?*

And how shall they hear without a preacher?" Our prayers are very good, but how often do we look for opportunities to share the Gospel?

God has given us dominion here on earth and He expects us to use it to bring about change in our society. Enough sitting on the sidelines, it's time to make a difference. It's time to take our stand! We pray for the poor, but what do we do about it? It's time to take action that will bring glory to God.

PRAY:

Lord, give me the strategies to express my faith, and the boldness to do what You show or tell me.

I pray that the love of God will fill me that many may experience His love through me.

James 2
Hebrews 10

16

HIS WORD AT WORK IN ME

"For as the rain comes down, and the snow from heaven, and do not return there, but water the earth, and make it bring forth and bud, That it may give seed to the sower and bread to the eater, so shall My word be that goes forth from My mouth; It shall not return to Me void, but it shall accomplish what I please, and it shall prosper in the thing for which I sent it."
(Isaiah 55:10-11)

I say "Amen" to this! The word of God is alive and powerful. It has creative power in it to cause us to become what His mouth has spoken. God's word can change a man's life in an instant or through a process. You can go to sleep poor and be a millionaire the next day. You can go to sleep not prophesying, the next day you can't stop prophesying. Even when we don't see it God's word is at work in our lives causing us and circumstances around us or situations that concern us to align with it. Isaiah 55:8-9 says, *"For My thoughts are not your thoughts, nor are your ways My ways, says the LORD. For as the heavens are higher than the earth, so are My ways higher than your ways, and My thoughts than your thoughts."*

The way in which God's word will be fulfilled is not

predictable — this means that we cannot determine how it will work in our lives. It does as God pleases and accomplishes what He wants. God may speak the same word to two people and the word will work differently in their lives to bring them to the same destination. One may wake up and become, while the other may go through a process to become. One thing is guaranteed, if God spoke it, then it is so. He is incapable of lying — He is not a man! To understand the magnitude of His word, Jesus Christ Himself is called the Word of God. So I can go to sleep tonight knowing that He is working it out for me according to His good purpose, and you never know, tomorrow my change may come.

So do not wait to see it till you believe, but believe it and you shall see it. *"For without faith it is impossible to please Him…" (Hebrews 11:6).*

PRAY:

Lord as I go to bed tonight, please do a work in me and for me that will transform my life for good.

Lord let there be an activation of all the gifts and calling you have deposited in me.

Ezekiel 37
1 Corinthians 12:1-11

17
I HAVE A TESTIMONY

> *"So the great dragon was cast out, that serpent of old, called the Devil and Satan, who deceives the whole world; he was cast to the earth, and his angels were cast out with him. Then I heard a loud voice saying in heaven, "Now salvation, and strength, and the kingdom of our God, and the power of His Christ have come, for the accuser of our brethren, who accused them before our God day and night, has been cast down. And they overcame him by the blood of the Lamb and by the word of their testimony, and they did not love their lives to the death."*
> *(Revelation 12:9-11)*

I have a testimony! Many times we feel testimonies have to be in the "big" or the "dramatic" things, but I believe testimonies are also in the things that the Lord did not allow us to pass through. For instance, the absolute fact that I did not get to the brink of death to be delivered is a testimony of God's faithfulness. Psalm 91:11 says that He will give His angels charge over us to keep us in all our ways and He has. The Scripture also says in Hebrews 12:24 (NLT) that *"You have come to Jesus, the one who mediates the new covenant between God and people, and to the sprinkled blood, which speaks of forgiveness instead of crying out for vengeance like the blood of Abel."* And truly it is so. If it were not so, then I would have been totally and utterly smashed by the devil.

He hides me under the shadow of His wings and stills my heart when I am anxious, in line His word in Philippians 4:6-7. He has blessed me even when curses were screaming out for me, His blood said "No" — Praise God! He has brought me through oppressing times and surrounds me with songs of deliverance and victory all around. Psalm 32:7 (NLT) says, *"For you are my hiding place; you protect me from trouble. You surround me with songs of victory"* Thank You Jesus, thank You my Lord.

PRAY:

Father, I thank You so much for always watching over me and being with me as I journey through life. Thank You for the things You have saved me from that I didn't even know about.

Thank You Lord for not allowing the storms of life to drown me.

Psalm 27
John 16

18

DETERMINED TO SUCCEED

"I can do all things through Christ who strengthens me"
(Philippians 4:13)

Being so used to driving on the right side of the road, it took me many years to get the courage to drive in England on the left side, but I eventually rose to the daunting task and I passed my driving test the second time around. I didn't do too well on my first manoeuvre, which was reversing round the corner, but I was determined not to let it distract or deflate me. I kept silently asking the Lord to help me keep calm. Unlike my very first test a couple of months back when after I made a mistake it unnerved me, and I kept telling myself over and over again in my head that I had failed the test, and I sure did.

My attitude going into the second test was different. Yes, I was nervous, but I decided from the onset that I was not going to let any mistake hinder me. I purposed just to drive as though I was merely carrying a passenger in the car, who was giving directions to a destination and not the Examiner. The same way as in life we must not let our mistakes hinder us or deter us from achieving the goal set before us. We must always rise above our mistakes, repenting where necessary and asking for God's help to move on.

Proverbs 24:16 says: *For a righteous man may fall seven times and rise again..."* and Psalm 37:23-24 *"The steps of a good man are ordered by the LORD, and He delights in his way. Though he fall, he shall not be utterly cast down; for the LORD upholds him with His hand."* These scriptures say it all, do not give up — it's not over till God says so.

PRAY:

Lord grant to me supernatural ability to function as I ought to in Jesus' name.

Open my eyes to see You Lord and to understand the instructions You are giving me in this season of my life.

Luke 8:40-56
Mark 10:46-52

19

LIVE FOR HIM

"He who has My commandments and keeps them, it is he who loves Me. And he who loves Me will be loved by My Father, and I will love him and manifest Myself to him."
(John 14:21)

I start this note with "I love you Jesus." It's something I say a lot. Could it be that at times I say it to convince myself that I do? Or possibly the more I say it the more I really get to love Him? I don't think so! I believe I say it simply to express my heartfelt adoration for Him. I know that I really do love Him and I live for Him and because of Him. If not for Him I know that I might not be alive today, and if alive I hate to imagine what my state would have been like. I do not want any other life apart from this — I live to serve Him and to do His will.

The song, "Because He lives, I can Face Tomorrow" by Gloria and William J. Gaither is so real to me, because each day I need His grace to make it through, for many times I can't see the way and I just have to walk by faith knowing that He is right beside me and cares what happens to me.

He really is very good to me, and at times I feel like His

favourite child. Yes, He chastens me when I'm naughty, but I like that because it has made me a better person, and of course He cuddles me with His Presence afterwards. This way I don't get complacent and live life anyhow that takes my fancy, instead I live life with the awareness that He is with me — He sees everything I do, He hears all I say, He knows my every thought, He knows it all.

PRAY:

Lord, I love You. Grant me the grace to love You more and to be totally sold out to You.

Lord help me to live for You as I should.

John 15
Galatians 5

20

TO BE CHILDLIKE AGAIN

"Assuredly, I say to you, whoever does not receive the kingdom of God as a little child will by no means enter it."
(Mark 10:15)

I first gave my life to Christ at a crusade, however though I loved the Lord and went to Church, my life went on as usual because I was never really told what was expected of me, and if I was told I obviously didn't understand. So I would still go to my drinking parties and carried on in my sin. After a while I moved from the city I was living in to another and stopped going to church regularly.

Three years down the line I went to a mid-week service with a cousin and answered the altar call again; this time it was for real, I understood what I was doing. For me this was when I truly became born again. I stumbled a bit at the onset because I didn't have good guidance from those around me, however I got back on the right track and completely lived for Him.

As a "babe" in the Lord, I fully trusted Him and took Him at His word. I read in the Bible that He works in me both to will and to do for His good pleasure *(Philippians 2:13)*; and I would pray that He would do so for me. I grew quickly in the Lord and every time I would look back, I would see the changes in me, and how He had answered my prayers. When I grew older in the Lord, I began to imagine that I was wiser and could work my way to where God wanted me to be — Wrong!

I'm learning to submit to God again as at the beginning and allowing Him to do His work in me. I want to be childlike again in my faith in the Lord (not childish though). When He says something, I want to simply believe that it will be as He has spoken. We can mature in Christ and still not lose this childlike quality (Matthew 18:3). The problem I feel is that when we grow in Christ we sometimes explain things away or become so familiar with Him and feel we understand Him so well and box Him out. We preach about His greatness, but in our own lives do we really understand the magnitude of this greatness?

I could go on and on, but I must stop here and ask you this question, "How do you see Him?"

PRAY:

Father, in anyway I have made You small in my thinking, please forgive me, help me to understand the magnitude of Your person.

Lord, inspire me by Your Spirit to understand Your word as I read, study and meditate on it.

Genesis 22:1-19
Joshua 6

21

BEING THANKFUL

"In everything give thanks; for this is the will of God in Christ Jesus for you."
(I Thessalonians 5:18)

I always have to take time to thank God again for the manifestation of His power not only in my life, but through my life also, because there are so many times when we are expecting a major breakthrough from the Lord, that we fail to see the seemingly "little things" that He is doing. However, if we would truly reflect upon our lives, I'm sure we'll see the hand of God at work somewhere. There might be a few people who might say "I really can't see anything," but the truth is that the fact that your problems have not killed you yet is because of the grace of God.

There are so many people that do not know Jesus Christ who go through the same trials, but because they do not have hope for a better tomorrow, their lives are destroyed. If we would only be still at times and allow the Lord to help us through the difficulties and trials that we face, the quicker the results we'll see. Whatever we go through we have to know that He truly loves us and His desire is not to harm us, but to do us good. We only have one life to live, so we must purpose to live a righteous life filled with His peace and joy. Romans 14:17 says, *"For the kingdom of God is not eating and drinking, but righteousness and peace and joy in the Holy Spirit."*

Whatever we desire that is of eternal value can only be acquired in Him, so *"Delight yourself also in the Lord, and He shall give you the desires of your heart"* (Psalm 37:4). I guess the question is how can we be still in the face of adversity? If there is nothing that we can do about it, why fret? It only leads to harm. Philippians 4:6 says, *"Be anxious for nothing, but in everything by prayer and supplication, with thanksgiving, let your requests be made known to God; and the peace of God, which surpasses all understanding, will guard your hearts and minds through Christ Jesus."*

Being "still" in God is not passive, but can be defined as not fretting but turning to God instead in prayer and supplication with thanksgiving, believing that grace would be made available to us to either to go through what we are going through or to meet us at our point of need. This may sound easier said than done, but thank God for the Holy Spirit who helps us in our weaknesses.

Think about this, who would you rather give to? The ungrateful person who always complains and nags you for more or the one who is grateful for even the "little'" that you've done for them? So even in what you are going through, still be thankful to God, let Him know that you love and appreciate Him, then ask Him for help.

PRAY:

Lord I really thank You for Your faithfulness in my life, and for having mercy on me when I'm ungrateful. I thank You also for all that You have done for me, and most especially for who You are to me.

(Pray for your needs — Psalm 62:8 says "Trust in Him at all times, you people; pour out your heart before Him; God is a refuge for us.")

Colossians 1
Psalm 9

22

I HAVE DONE IT AGAIN!

"Even a fool is counted wise when he holds his peace; when he shuts his lips, he is considered perceptive."
(Proverbs 17:28)

The very thing that I do not want to do, I do and that which I wish to do, I don't. What is this thing? It is getting involved in pointless debates or arguments that lead nowhere, or at least do not matter. It just gets me hot under the collar and it leaves me feeling bad afterwards. There are some people who are able to have passionate debates about issues and it doesn't affect them much, but not so with me — especially when I feel it's not going my way.

My father gave me a Bible of his called the Jerusalem Bible a year or two before he went to be with the Lord, and I love how it puts 2 Timothy 2:23-25, *"Avoid those futile and silly speculations, understanding that they only give rise to quarrels; and a servant of the Lord is not to engage in quarrels, but has to be kind to everyone, a good teacher and patient. He has to be gentle when he corrects people who dispute what he says, never forgetting that God may give them a change of mind..."*

I have come to realise that I don't always have to be right about everything and to be still in God; being quick to listen and slow to speak as His word advises me to in James 1:19. There are certain times though that I know that I must speak, but at these times I feel the grace of God with me and the Holy Spirit inspiring me to speak, still I let my words be few lest I get carried away and say more than I ought. Proverbs 17:27-28 says in the NIV version, *"The one who has knowledge uses words with restraint, and whoever has understanding is even-tempered. Even fools are thought wise if they keep silent, and discerning if they hold their tongues."*

I thank God that I am much better now, however, even the once in a while that I stumble on this issue annoys me. Oh I wish I were perfect and never did anything wrong. Thank God for His grace and mercy.

PRAY:

Lord, set a guard over my mouth and keep the door of my lips (Psalm 141:3).

Give me the tongue of the learned, that I may know how to speak a word in season (Isaiah 50:4)

Romans 7
Psalm 19

23

HE THAT IS IN ME

"Or do you not know that your body is the temple of the Holy Spirit who is in you, whom you have from God, and you are not your own? For you were bought at a price; therefore glorify God in your body and in your spirit, which are God's."
(1 Corinthians 6:19-20)

What does the above scripture mean to me?
- That the Holy Spirit is not only with me, but also most importantly is in me. So then I don't need to rely on my own abilities, but I must yield to Him to work in me and through me.
- The Holy Spirit in me is greater than anyone in the world; therefore I must always be aware of this great power within me.
- Because He dwells in me, I must take care what I do with my body and the thoughts that I entertain.
- I have power within me to help me live a godly life and to glorify God in everything.
- I have the realm of the supernatural available to me.
- I am not my own, so I simply cannot do whatever takes my fancy.
- I do not just up and go and expect the Holy Spirit not to

have a say on where I go or what I do.
- I need to be more yielded to Him, because He is in me to accomplish God's purpose in my life and to help me to live the life of an "overcomer" here on earth.
- "The Spirit is God's guarantee that he will give us the inheritance he promised and that he has purchased us to be his own people. He did this so we would praise and glorify him." (Ephesians 1:14 NIV)

PRAY:

Dear Holy Spirit, help me to yield to You, instruct me, teach me, lead me in the way I should go (Psalm 32:8).

Lord, fill me till I overflow and help me to walk in Your supernatural power.

Romans 8
2 Corinthians 3

24

FOR GOD'S SAKE

"The young lions lack and suffer hunger;
but those who seek the LORD shall not lack any good thing."
(Psalm 34:10)

I've known a few people testify that when they first gave their hearts to Christ, it was as though the Lord could not stop blessing them (maybe I should say pampering them), it happened to me too; but as they got older in Christ it seemed not that simple. There could be many reasons for this: we know that as we grow in the Lord, we come to a place where we realise or must come to realise that *"man cannot live by bread alone, but by every word that proceeds from the mouth of God."* (Matthew 4:4). We also know that or should know that the "waiting" period of our lives is working something of eternal value in us — it builds endurance, it builds character in us. As we mature in the Lord, God also trains our hands to war, not physical war but spiritual war, as we go deep in the word and learn how to pray effectively and fervently.

Another reason could also be that when some of us first gave our hearts to the Lord, we had eyes only for Him, but along the way, other things began to take our fancy and slowly, though we still loved the Lord and were in Christ, we sought more for the things we could get from Him, rather than Him. These things may not be necessarily bad; it could be His power, His favour, signs and wonders, money, a spouse, ministry, to mention but a few. Our eyes can be so fixed on these things that we ignore what is more essential, and that is our relationship with Him. As we begin to drift off we may not know it, but He is calling us back to our first love.

James 4:3 says, *"You ask and do not receive, because you ask amiss, that you may spend it on your pleasures."* God has blessed us and wants to bless us some more, but in the right order. Jesus says in Matthew 6:31-33 *"Therefore do not worry, saying, 'What shall we eat?' or 'What shall we drink?' or 'What shall we wear?' For after all these things the Gentiles seek. For your heavenly Father knows that you need all these things. But seek first the kingdom of God and His righteousness, and all these things shall be added to you."* So as we go deeper into Him, we will have access to the things that we really need.

Are we seeking after God simply for the things He can give us? Or maybe even for just the things that He can do through us, rather than seeking after God for God Himself — so that even if He doesn't answer our prayers when we want or as we want, we still love Him. I'd rather my husband love me for me rather than for what I do for him, because it means that when I can no longer do those things then he can fall out of love with me. However, if he loves me for me, the things that I do are just bonuses that possibly make him appreciate me the more.

If we seek after God only for the goodies that He gives then we might get frustrated, because He is not a "puppet–on–a–string" that we can pull whenever we want. In fact if this is the case, the more likely that the Lord will allow us to be frustrated, because maybe in our frustration we can truly search for Him. It's an honour to be called His children, not the other way round – Let's not forget this!

PRAY:

Lord, I return to You, I open up my heart to You, use my life for Your glory.

Lord, I'm sorry for having elevated the things that I desire more than my desire for You. I want You to be my first love.

Zechariah 1
Deuteronomy 10

25

I CAN WAKE UP TO CHANGE

"Now indeed, Elizabeth your relative has also conceived a son in her old age; and this is now the sixth month for her who was called barren. For with God nothing will be impossible."
(Luke 1:36-37)

I can wake up in the morning and be changed. I may be able to do what I couldn't do before in line with His purpose for my life. Things that had been impossible for me before, suddenly become possible, because their season have come. The enemies of progress that I see today, tomorrow I'll see them no more. Suddenly lack will be gone and abundance will become the reality of my life!

All things can happen as I wake up in the morning, because the dawn of a new day may open up for me a dawn of greatness. More importantly, I can wake up knowing God better and having a deeper revelation of Him. The scriptures can become open to me in new ways and I can begin to understand deeper things of God, because tonight God can visit me and with His touch change my life forever. He is after all, the Creator, the Most High God. Furthermore He has been working in my life and I simply yield to Him to make me what He wants me to be. Everyday it's becoming more glaring that I'm useless without Him.

So, I'll simply walk with Him day by day, pray a lot, eat His word, do whatever He lays on my heart to do and do the good I know to do and as Job said in Job 14:14 "... *I'll wait till my change comes.*" His word never fails; it tells me that He is able to accomplish much more that I can ask or imagine because of His great power at work in me (Ephesians 3:20). Hallelujah!

PRAY:

Lord, show me Your ways so that I may walk with You better.

Lord, I pray for wisdom and understanding so I may know how to prepare in this season of my life, so that I can be positioned for the changes that I desire and the changes that you want to work in my life.

2 Kings 6
2 Kings 7

26

A GOD OF PURPOSE

"And He has made from one blood every nation of men to dwell on all the face of the earth, and has determined their preappointed times and the boundaries of their dwellings, so that they should seek the Lord, in the hope that they might grope for Him and find Him, though He is not far from each one of us; for in Him we live and move and have our being, as also some of your own poets have said, 'For we are also His offspring.'"
(Acts 17:26-28)

God truly is a God of purpose and is long-suffering towards us. He could have used anyone other than Moses to bring the people of Israel out of Egypt, however He didn't take "no" for an answer, because that was what He had prepared Moses for, from birth. Even when Moses asked Him to use someone else because he felt inadequate; he felt that he was not a man of eloquent speech, the Lord insisted that He had to be the one. Exodus 4:10 NLT says, *"But Moses pleaded with the Lord, "O Lord, I'm not very good with words. I never have been, and I'm not now, even though you have spoken to me. I get tongue-tied, and my words get tangled."*

Moses wasn't exactly dumb or clueless, but maybe lacked

confidence in his own abilities. Stephen says in Acts 7:22 NLT *"Moses was taught all the wisdom of the Egyptians, and he was powerful in both speech and action."* So the Lord allowed him to have his brother Aaron who could speak well to help him. God said to Moses concerning Aaron *"Talk to him, and put the words in his mouth. I will be with both of you as you speak, and I will instruct you both in what to do. Aaron will be your spokesman to the people. He will be your mouthpiece, and you will stand in the place of God for him, telling him what to say."* (Exodus 4:15-16 NLT).

Obviously Aaron did not do all the talking throughout their time together, Moses did a fair bit too as we can see In Numbers 12:2 NLT when Miriam and Aaron were speaking against Moses *"They said, "Has the Lord spoken only through Moses? Hasn't he spoken through us, too?" But the Lord heard them."*

This gives me confidence that what God has written concerning my life, He will bring to pass. Wherever I'm lacking confidence or resources He is able to help me or bring divine helpers to aid me. All I have been through and the things I've done or not done, can all work together to bring me to the point of destiny. Even when I miss it, once I get myself back in His hands and in His will, He will steer me back to the right path. What a faithful God we serve!

Be encouraged, whatever you are going through or have been through, good can still come out of it. His word to you is in Romans 8:28 *"And we know that all things work together for good to those who love God, to those who are the called according to His purpose."* So make sure you are in the Master's Hand and that He is at the centre of all you are and all you do.

PRAY:

Lord let good come out of every negative thing I'm going through or I've been through.

I yield to You O Lord, transform my heart to do Your will. Help me to understand what You are doing in my life in this season and help me to cooperate with your plan for my life.

Exodus 4
Psalm 139

27

NO ONE CAN REVERSE HIS WORKS

"God is not a man, that He should lie, nor a son of man, that He should repent. Has He said, and will He not do? Or has He spoken, and will He not make it good? Behold, I have received a command to bless; He has blessed, and I cannot reverse it."
(Numbers 23:19-20)

In the account in the book of Exodus from chapter seven, we can see that the enemy's power is limited. When Aaron threw down his rod and it became a serpent, the magicians of Pharaoh each threw down their rods and they became serpents also, however, Aaron's serpent being more superior to theirs swallowed them all up.

Again Moses told Aaron to stretch forth his rod and all the rivers and waters in Egypt became blood and the fish in the waters died and there was no drinking water for the people. Pharaoh called on his magicians for help and all they could do was make matters worse by doing the same thing, but they could not reverse what the Lord had done. Then came the frogs, the magicians could also not make the frogs disappear, they only made matters worse again for themselves by calling out more frogs. Pharaoh had to plead with Moses to make the frogs disappear when he realised their magic was limited. After the frogs came the lice, the magicians could not duplicate this and the others that followed. God delivered His people from Egypt with many signs and wonders to reveal Himself to them.

This tells me that when God speaks no one can reverse it (certainly not the devil), when He stretches forth His hand, no one can pull it back. The devil can't stop God's word or work in our lives, however he does try to stop us entering into the "Promised Land" through sin, discouragement, fear, strife, contention and the like. He tried to discourage Moses and Aaron by "showing off" his own power, but they had a revelation of God and knew that the battle was already won — victory was theirs! Glory to God!

The Bible says the devil goes about like a roaring lion seeking whom he may devour, but we have been enjoined to submit to God, resist the devil and be strong in our faith (1 Peter 5:8; James 4:7). Ephesians 6:11 says, *"Put on the whole armor of God, that you may be able to stand against the wiles of the devil."* (See Ephesians 6:13-18 for the list of the various components of this armour.)

PRAY:

Lord, strengthen me where I am weak and let Your word prevail in my life. Help me to stand firm in faith as my roots go deep in Your love. May I know You more and more and be filled with Your fullness.

Father, in the name of Jesus Christ I submit to You and resist the devil and according to Your word He must flee from me.

Numbers 23
1 Peter 5

28

DON'T BE SOMEONE ELSE

"From the place of His dwelling He looks on all the inhabitants of the earth; He fashions their hearts individually; He considers all their works".
(Psalm 33:14-15)

God has made me unique, He has fashioned my heart after His purpose for my life. Everything that I should do He has planted in my heart, those things that will bring me fulfilment, things that are after His divine purpose. I cannot afford to try to be like anyone else, or act like somehow else, except of course to emulate godly attributes that I see in other people. My expression of service to Him must be in line with what He has fashioned for me.

Poor Moses, what mental torture He endured from the people he was leading. It's amazing that people like Korah, Dathan, Abiram an On in Numbers sixteen could be envious of his position. Instead of being the best at what they were called to do, they envied another's calling. They only saw the honour of the position and not the down side of leading such grumblers, but because this was Moses' purpose and because he was intimate with the living God, he had the grace to bear it or should I say endure it. Many times God wanted to destroy the people, but Moses would intercede for them. At the end though, Moses got so irritated with the people that he erred against God and was not allowed to enter the Promised Land till his death.

Korah, along with Dathan and Abiram with their wives and children were all destroyed for conspiring against Moses and rebelling against God. However Korah's sons did not die that day (the prophet Samuel was from the lineage of Korah). Another lesson that can be learned from this is not to follow people to do evil. You might end up with the egg on your face. Numbers 26:9-11 NLT says *"and Eliab was the father of Nemuel, Dathan, and Abiram. This Dathan and Abiram are the same community leaders who conspired with Korah against Moses and Aaron, rebelling against the LORD. But the earth opened up its mouth and swallowed them with Korah, and fire devoured 250 of their followers. This served as a warning to the entire nation of Israel. However, the sons of Korah did not die that day."*

Trying to be who you are not called to be can destroy you emotionally, if not physically, because you are not anointed for it. Be who you were created to be, be the best "you" that you can be. Allow God to work in you to bring out the depths of treasure(s) in you. You were created for a purpose. Psalm 139:13-16 says: *"For You formed my inward parts; You covered me in my mother's womb. I will praise You, for I am fearfully and wonderfully made; marvelous are Your works, and that my soul knows very well. My frame was not hidden from You, when I was made in secret, and skillfully wrought in the lowest parts of the earth. Your eyes saw my substance, being yet unformed. And in Your book they all were written, the days fashioned for me, when as yet there were none of them."*

The way you are is what God has used and will use to qualify you, but unfortunately, these very traits that are meant to be a blessing the devil corrupts and uses negatively to disqualify you. The devil tries to pollute the desires and traits that God has put in us in different ways; like through confusion, enticing one to do evil or getting our focus on to other things. Let us examine ourselves and get rid of the junk that may hinder us from coming into what He Has laid up for us. Psalm 19:12-13 says, *"Who can understand his errors? Cleanse me from secret faults. Keep back your servant also from presumptuous sins; let them not have dominion over me. Then I shall be blameless, and I shall be innocent of great transgression."*

Run your own race! You are special, you are unique, like a piece of a jigsaw puzzle, if a little piece is missing, the puzzle will not be complete. Sufficient are the trials and testing you have to endure in your own race, there's no need adding to it. Furthermore, the most important thing is doing what God has called you to do, because this is what He has given you the grace for. Remember service without intimacy is just works, but service that comes from a place of intimacy yields fruit, fruit that remains. So while I wait for the bigger picture, I will do what I find to do, till He steers my heart onto the greater things that He has for me.

PRAY:

Lord, uproot every seed in my life that you have not planted. May seeds that corrupt who You have made me to be not flourish in my life. Help me to abide in You and You in me so that I can bear much fruit (John 15:5).

Help me to see myself as You see me and to know and value Your calling for my life.

Exodus 36
1 Corinthians 12:12-31

29

GOING ALL THE WAY

"Have you not known? Have you not heard? The everlasting God, the LORD, The Creator of the ends of the earth, neither faints nor is weary. His understanding is unsearchable. He gives power to the weak, and to those who have no might He increases strength."
(Isaiah 40:28-29)

Are you determined to go all the way? Looking at the account in Luke chapter 5:17-26 (The cure of a paralytic), what would have happened if they didn't go all the way? What if they had felt defeated by their inability to go in through the main entrance to lay the paralytic man at the feet of Jesus? What if the paralytic himself had lost hope and allowed the bumps and maybe the bruises of trying to get him up onto the roof and then lowering him down into the house to discourage him?

Do you have faith to go all the way? Are you prepared to fight the good fight of faith (1 Timothy 6:12), not giving up no matter the bumps and the bruises, trusting that God has the power to deliver you and that He will see you through to the end? Jesus Christ was unable to do much in His hometown because the people did not receive Him. Even in church today, many are struggling to believe and we still live defeated lives when this ought not to be so.

Have we made the Lord too small in our eyes, or do we believe that the exchange at the Cross is only for some and not for all who receive Him? I love the resolve of the woman with the issue of blood in Mark 5:25-34, this is what I believe she thought, "If He doesn't touch me, I'll touch Him," so she reached out with all determination to touch His garment. She must have had to push to get through the crowd, but that didn't deter her, frail as she might have been. Blind Bartimaeus is another example in Mark 10:46-52; he refused to let people hinder him from getting his breakthrough. They did their best to shut him up, but he shouted all the more.

What about you? Even if God is taking you through a process, He doesn't expect you to just sit still and do nothing. When He says, "be still," He is saying, "do not fret" — you must praise, you must worship, you must meditate on and declare the word of God and you must pray all manner of prayers and take every necessary action. Let the Holy Spirit inspire you; if it is a process, as you pray He is able to change you or give you divine insight to change the situation. If it is a demonic problem, He is able to deliver you; even if it's a miracle you need, He is able to work it out for you. I leave you with the words of the Lord in Luke 18 verses 1-8: *"Then He spoke a parable to them, that men always ought to pray and not lose heart, saying: "There was in a certain city a judge who did not fear God nor regard man. Now there was a widow in that city; and she came to him, saying, 'Get justice for me from my adversary.' And he would not for a while; but afterward he said within himself, 'Though I do not fear God nor regard man, yet because this widow troubles me I will avenge her, lest by her continual coming she weary me.' "Then the Lord said, "Hear what the unjust judge said. And shall God not avenge His own elect who cry out day and night to Him, though He bears long with them? I tell you that He will avenge them speedily. Nevertheless, when the Son of Man comes, will He really find faith on the earth?""*

PRAY:

Lord, please revive Your works in my life and grant me the grace that I need to fight the good fight of faith.

Cause me to mount up with wings as eagles and not be weary or faint.

2 Kings 13:14-20
Revelations 12

30

HIS VESSEL

"This is what the Lord says — your Redeemer, who formed you in the womb: I am the Lord, the Maker of all things, who stretches out the heavens, who spreads out the earth by myself,"
(Isaiah 44:24 NIV)

God truly does use the foolish things of the world to confound the wise, and I am an example of His mercy and grace. I really am not versed in public speaking and my oral English is just about average, because at times I believe it takes me a while to decode messages in my brain (or so it seems to me), but listening to some messages that I have preached I am truly amazed. Words I would not normally use, I used; my spoken English sounded good, and to add to this I preached with boldness. I was amazed at what I heard. You may not understand how I feel, but I know that it is the Spirit of God at work in me.

I know without a doubt that it is the anointing, the Holy Spirit supplying the words and using me as a vessel to deliver His word. I remember in college I used to avoid taking classes that required me to give oral presentations, and when I had to, without fail I used to fall flat on my face. Even now I still get a bit jittery about speaking in public, but I'm encouraged by what God told Moses in Exodus 4:11-12 when he was trying to dodge his assignment because he felt he could not speak effectively: *"So the LORD said to him, "Who has made man's mouth? Or who makes the mute, the deaf, the seeing, or the blind? Have not I, the LORD? Now therefore, go, and I will be with your mouth and teach you what you shall say."* This is exactly what He has and still does for me.

So fear not! Whatever He calls you to do, He equips you for. Just walk with Him by faith, putting your trust in Him—the I AM, the One who is the Almighty, the Creator of the heavens and the earth and all things seen and unseen. So read, study and meditate on the word, pray, praise and worship Him. He is more than able to make you what He wants you to be as you totally surrender to Him.

PRAY:

Lord, I yield to You in total submission. I pledge my allegiance to you completely.

Let Your gifts and calling for my life begin to manifest that all may know that it's You at work in me.

1 Corinthians 1
1 Corinthians 2

31

HOW DO YOU SEE HIM?

"But without faith it is impossible to please Him, for he who comes to God must believe that He is, and that He is a rewarder of those who diligently seek Him."
(Hebrews 11:6)

Some limitations and struggles that we have in our lives as Christians are derived from the way we see God. Some see Him as a "Sugar Daddy" that just doles out the gifts whenever they ask, so at the first glimpse of any challenge, they faint or backslide. Some see Him as "Love" and this He is, however they forget that because He loves us He disciplines us (for our own good). So they go about their merry way doing whatever they please without regard to the consequences of their actions. Others see Him simply as a "Task Master" who delights in punishing them for no reason. If we have the wrong perception of Him, then our walk with Him will be greatly hindered. That's why it's so crucial that we seek to know Him.

Who is He to you? Not simply that He is God, but what is your perception of Him and better still, how is your relationship with Him? If we truly know Him, then all our problems will pale into insignificance before Him — because then we may realise that He is bigger than all our problems put together and more importantly He is able to do something about them. The last part of Daniel 11:32 says *"...but the people who know their God shall be strong, and carry out great exploits."*

You are indeed very special to Him. 1 Peter 2:9-10 says, *"But you are a chosen generation, a royal priesthood, a holy nation, His own special people, that you may proclaim the praises of Him who called you out of darkness into His marvelous light; who once were not a people but are now the people of God, who had not obtained mercy but now have obtained mercy."* He paid a costly price for you with the blood of His only begotten Son. Through this sacrifice He has also given to us the Spirit of adoption (Romans 8:15) so we can call Him Father. So if He is our Father, then we ought to have an intimate relationship with Him, and even when He does discipline us, we should know it's for our own good (Hebrews 12:6), because we are assured that He loves us and His thoughts towards us and His plans for us are good ones.

PRAY:

Lord I pray that my life will be flooded with light, so that I can understand the confident hope You have given to those you called (Ephesians 1;18)

Forgive me for not valuing You as I ought to.

Isaiah 40:12-31
Isaiah 43

32

HE IS WORKING ON US

"But we all, with unveiled face, beholding as in a mirror the glory of the Lord, are being transformed into the same image from glory to glory, just as by the Spirit of the Lord."
(2 Corinthians 3:18)

At times we feel as though there is still a lot of work to be done in our lives. However if we look back over the years, we would see how far He has brought us, and the changes He has made in our lives. Even if you've just given your life to Christ, the Holy Spirit is working in you as you submit to Him. We must thank Him for this, while waiting for more change.

If you cannot see any change in your life for the better when you reflect on your life, then there must be a problem that you need to ask the Lord to reveal to you. Maybe changes you have to make in your life or certain truths you need to know or appropriate. One thing we must know is that when we are yielded to Him, even though we may struggle at times, everyday He is working on us and for us, and will cause all things to work together for our good as His word says in Romans 8:28, *"And we know [with great confidence] that*

God [who is deeply concerned about us] causes all things to work together [as a plan] for good for those who love God, to those who are called according to His plan and purpose." (AMP)

In Christ, the devil no longer has the right to torment us; however, he is really crafty and does still try to find access into our lives, looking for wherever there is a break in the hedge. Whether through our ignorance we give him room, through sin, through fear, through negative pronouncements, through curses, demonic objects that we keep in our homes, maybe even through things that we watch or read that glorify him. Thanks be to our God that we have the victory through Jesus Christ. Jesus Christ is the Mediator of the new covenant and His blood is speaking better things concerning us, because we have redemption and forgiveness through His blood (Ephesians 1:7), so even if the devil does assail us because of sin, when we confess our sins and repent, getting rid of any demonic objects that we may have, we are able to order him out and reclaim lost ground. Whatever the reason for the attack, the blood of Jesus is powerful. Revelations 12:11 says *"And they overcame him by the blood of the Lamb and by the word of their testimony, and they did not love their lives to the death."*

PRAY:

Lord help me to see and appreciate the changes you have made in my life and to be thankful for this.

Lord what must I do to get to the next level? I surrender all of me to You — spirit, soul and body. Help me to know Your heart and to walk with You daily.

Luke 6:37-49
Philippians 2

33

REST IN HIM

"Let us therefore be diligent to enter that rest, lest anyone fall according to the same example of disobedience."
(Hebrews 4:11)

Many times we treat unbelief lightly, however Hebrews 3:18-19 likens it to disobedience and says, *"And to whom did He swear that they would not enter His rest, but to those who did not obey? So we see that they could not enter in because of unbelief."* Could this be the reason why so many are struggling? Are they finding it hard to truly believe that He is who He is, that He can do what He says He can do, or that He will do what He says He will do?

One sure way to rest in Him is found in 1 Timothy 6:6-8 which says that, *"Now godliness with contentment is great gain. For we brought nothing into this world, and it is certain we can carry nothing out. And having food and clothing, with these we shall be content."* This way whether we have in abundance or we lack, we are still in God's rest. Being content does not mean that we cannot desire more, certainly not! We can desire more and pray for more, but we must not let our desires consume us to the point that it steals our peace or make us compromise our beliefs and when we do get more, it is not to squander it on our pleasures by acquiring lots and lots of possessions for ourselves or living a life of debauchery, but it is to bring glory to Him and also be a blessing to those in need and to fund the work of His Kingdom.

We must trust God and be thankful for what we have, while we wait for the "extra" that He has for us. We must wait patiently for the Lord and do whatever He says to do whether we see the promise or not, for it is in these "waiting times" that character is built in us. James 1:4 says, *"but let patience have its perfect work, that you may be perfect and complete, lacking nothing."* And Hebrews 4:10 *"For he who has entered His rest has himself also ceased from his works as God did from His."* Therefore, we do not strive to get or scheme to get, but allow ourselves to be led by the Holy Spirit. The Holy Spirit knows what the mind of God is, because He is God and He knows all that we need and should have; and more importantly He knows what we must do to get these things and the timing.

"And God is able to bless you abundantly, so that in all things at all times, having all that you need, you will abound in every good work." (2 Corinthians 9:8 NIV). So rest in the fact that He is for you.

PRAY:

Lord, help me to enter into Your rest.

Teach me how to profit in life and give me the power I need to excel in all You've called me to be and to do.

James 1
Revelations 14

34

BE A BLESSING

"I will make you into a great nation. I will bless you and make you famous, and you will be a blessing to others."
(Genesis 12:2 NLT)

God wants to settle us, but in order to do this He needs to change us, or the circumstances around us, so that His blessings may enrich us and not destroy us and in turn we also can be a blessing to others. It's not God's desire that we are always suffering, always struggling — that is the devil's plan. The Lord wants us to have an abundant life, however this does not mean that we will not go through trials and tribulations, but in all things we should be more than conquerors; we should by God's grace be able to stand and not faint. Having said this, we must know that we should not be going through the same situation over and over again; if we are, something needs to change or something needs to be learned. Thank God that He is willing to show us what the problem is if we care to know, and if we open our hearts to receive what He is saying.

Whatever God does in our lives, He does so that in turn we may affect other lives. He builds us so that we can help build other lives; He delivers us so that we can help deliver others. We need to get this, so that we don't just live for ourselves, we need to look for ways to be a blessing to others, for the scriptures says, *"it is more blessed to give than to receive"* (Acts 20:35). God will always bless a generous heart, a heart that not only seeks to be blessed but to be a blessing. 2 Corinthians 1:3-4 says *"Blessed be the God and Father of our Lord Jesus Christ, the Father of mercies and God of all comfort, who comforts us in all our tribulation, that we may be able to comfort those who are in any trouble, with the comfort with which we ourselves are comforted by God."*

PRAY:

Lord, what should I do in this season? How can I be a blessing?

God of peace, I thank You for showering me with Your grace and mercy, I pray that grace and mercy will also flow through me to others.

Isaiah 61
2 Corinthians 1

35

HANDS OFF!

"And the Lord said, "Simon, Simon! Indeed, Satan has asked for you, that he may sift you as wheat. But I have prayed for you, that your faith should not fail; and when you have returned to Me, strengthen your brethren."
(Luke 22:31-32)

Don't you just wish at times that you could take your loved ones pains away, supply everything that they need so that they never have to worry or hurt. As a Pastor and parent, at times this is how I feel about the people that the Lord has brought into my life. Whenever they go through, it really gets to me and I wish I could do more about it than just pray, counsel them or do the bit that I can.

We cannot be God in anyone's life, we can only help as best as we can, making sure that we teach them kingdom principles to help them to stand on their own and develop their own intimate relationship with the Lord. Having done this, there comes a time that we might have to "hands off" so that their focus may be on God and not on us, and allow God to be God in their lives. It's very hard at times though when it seems as if the Lord is not showing up quickly enough, at least not in the way that we expect Him to. The truth is that we simply have to trust God and know that He loves them more than we can ever possibly do. If only we knew what God is doing in their lives it certainly would make it easier, but He usually doesn't say, or could it be that in some cases we don't really hear? One thing is for sure, and that is that He wants a personal relationship with them and there are certain things that they can only apprehend in the secret place, and when they come through, they will come out stronger; but when we keep meddling in their issues we may keep them from maturing and knowing God for themselves.

A dear friend (more like a big brother) who is with the Lord now used to say, "If you fix the fix that God has fixed to fix you, He will fix another fix to fix you." I'm not sure if it is an original saying of his, but it sure gets the message across. What we need to do more importantly at these times is to pray fervently for them and be there for them when they need a helping hand. I like what the Bible says about Epaphras in Colossians 4:12 (NLT) *"Epaphras, a member of your own fellowship and a servant of Christ Jesus, sends you his greetings. He always prays earnestly for you, asking God to make you strong and perfect, fully confident that you are following the whole will of God."* Let us follow his example and also pray earnestly for them, in addition to being as charitable as we can be.

PRAY:

Lord I lift... (insert name or names) before you today, please come to his/her rescue. (Pray for their known needs, pray that they will know God more intimately. Pray that they will mature in Christ fully pleasing Him in all things. Ask the Lord to reveal His will for their life/lives to them and show them whatever is in their life/lives that might be a source of hindrance to them.)

(Pray in tongues for them if you are able to, or ask the Holy Spirit to lay other prayers on your heart for them, then pray whatever comes to mind.)

Mark 2
1 Timothy 2:1-8

36

HE'S NOT PARTIAL

"And remember that the heavenly Father to whom you pray has no favorites. He will judge or reward you according to what you do. So you must live in reverent fear of him during your time here as "temporary residents.""
(1 Peter 1:17 NLT)

God does not show favouritism, neither does He take a bribe (Acts 10:34, Deuteronomy 10:17). When some people hear this, they simply don't believe it, because they compare themselves to other people and feel hard done by. Some people believe this, but live their lives in an ungodly manner and wonder why things are not as they should be. Acts 10:35, qualifies verse 34 by saying, *"but accepts men from every nation and tribe that fear Him and do what is right."* The word of God also says in Matthew 5:6 that those who hunger and thirst after righteousness shall be filled. You don't have to necessarily do what I do to experience the favour I have with God; all you have to do is do what He wants you to do.

Remember this, God is also a God of purpose and a God who keeps covenant, so don't fret if your life is not like the next person's. Allow God to work His purpose in your life and it will suit you perfectly, because it is what He fashioned out for you when you were being formed in your mother's womb (Psalm 139:13-17). Thank God He is no respecter of persons, but He is a just God. The Lord said to Judah in Isaiah 1:19 *"If you are willing and obedient, You shall eat the good of the land;"* So pursue the Lord, love and serve Him with all your heart, all my mind and all your strength and allow Him to perfect all that concerns you.

PRAY:

Our God of peace, You who brought up our Lord Jesus from the dead, the great Shepherd of the sheep, through the blood of the everlasting covenant, make me complete in every good work to do Your will, working in me what is well pleasing in Your sight, through Jesus Christ, to You be glory forever and ever — Amen! (Hebrews 13:20-21)

Lord reign in every area of my life.

1 Samuel 16
Deuteronomy 9

37

GOOD ENOUGH FOR GOD?

"For if our heart condemns us, God is greater than our heart, and knows all things."
(I John 3:20)

The devil always tries to put us under pressure and condemnation that we are not good enough for God to use. Thank God that righteousness was inputted to us, therefore this means that it is not by our works of righteousness (though we should walk in righteousness), but He has made us righteous through the sacrifice of our Lord Jesus Christ. Does this mean that we should be slack and sin? Of course not! Nevertheless, as the Scripture says, *"…all our righteousnesses are like filthy rags …"* (Isaiah 64:6), because what He requires is perfection, and in our own strength this is impossible to attain.

Jesus Christ came to pay the once and for all price for us — to save us. Ephesians 2:8-9 says *"For by grace you have been saved through faith, and that not of yourselves; it is the gift of God, not of works, lest anyone should boast."* God knew we were not perfect when he called us; that's why Christ shed His blood for us, so that even if we do stumble we have an advocate with the Father — Jesus Christ. So rather than buy into the lies of the devil, cultivate an intimate relationship with the Lord and by faith stand upon His completed works on the Cross of calvary.

Cultivating an intimate relationship with Him is not about praying five hours a day (wonderful if you can), but let it be "quality rather than just quantity" as the Lord once told me through a prophetic couple when I was pregnant with my second child. I used to struggle to pray for an hour a day; I was here, there and everywhere in my prayers, in and out of sleep — I came out of prayers feeling unfulfilled, never really connecting with Him as I desired. When I got this word it changed my prayer life then. I stopped struggling to simply put in an hour at once, but prayed as much as I could to connect with Him as often I could in the day and soon I began to enjoy my prayer time again.

As we spend quality time with Him, we will come to cherish these moments and want more of it. It will no longer feel like a chore, but pure joy that you wouldn't want to leave His presence and it is there in His presence that He is able to mould our hearts and empower us to become who He has created us to be. So be encouraged, if you feel like you are useless, you really are not once you are in His hands. God is able to use you no matter how inadequate you feel you are. He is in the business of using the foolish things of this world to confound the wise (1 Corinthians 1:26-29).

PRAY:

Lord help me to know the joy of Your Presence like I've never known it before.

I lift up my eyes to You Lord Jesus, the Author and Finisher of my faith (Hebrews 12:2).

1 Peter 2
Ephesians 1

38

HE KNOWS HOW TO SPEAK

"Your ears shall hear a word behind you, saying, "This is the way, walk in it," Whenever you turn to the right hand Or whenever you turn to the left."
(Isaiah 30:21)

I can't help but ponder at the awesomeness of our Father who meets our needs sometimes by touching people's hearts to be a blessing to us. The amazing thing is that people who may ordinarily say that they don't know the voice of God still hear Him one way or the other. Certainly God knows how to speak to everyone He needs to speak to, He'll use a mule if He has to (as in the case of Balaam in Numbers 22:28-30). May we not harden our hearts and refuse to obey Him when He speaks to us. However do test what you believe He is saying to you with the scriptures, He will not contradict His word — the Bible.

Proverbs 21:1 says, *"The king's heart is in the hand of the LORD, like the rivers of water; He turns it wherever He wishes."* I remember an incident when I had been complaining to my husband that my daughter needed clothes as she had outgrown most of her clothes, so I went out and bought her two tops, I was going to buy more with my credit card (because we were short on cash), but I felt the Lord say to wait, so I waited. The next day, a dear friend and sister in the Lord who had just come back from holiday, sent a minicab to us with bags of all sorts of clothes for my daughter. To add to this she put in two lovely suits for me. Isn't our God truly awesome? He knows how to add the "extras" to our desires or requests. Somehow He caused this wonderful woman to hear Him in order to meet my needs.

May He open our hearts to be a blessing to as many as He leads us to, and may those who He has raised up for us, do what He has put in their hearts and hands to do too.

PRAY:

Lord, let every good thing that you have for me today reach me.

Lord GOD please give me the tongue of the learned, that I may speak a word in season to him who is weary. Awaken me morning by morning, awaken my ear to hear as the learned. (Isaiah 50:4)

Numbers 22
1 Kings 17

39

GOD'S WORK IN PROGRESS

"Before I formed you in the womb I knew you; Before you were born I sanctified you; I ordained you a prophet to the nations."
(Jeremiah 1:5)

It is a good thing that we are not just God's work in process, but we are God's work in progress. A work can be in process and never really get completed or the process is more or less stagnant. Progress however can be defined as forward movement, growth, advancement, moving towards a goal. So we need to wake up and begin to live life not only as though we are going somewhere, but knowing that we truly are going somewhere. We need to expect victory! Some people are so used to defeat that they don't expect victory and of course if you don't expect it you may not get it or may not realise that you've got it even if it slaps you in the face.

Be focused on where you are going; the expected end that God has shown you or told you about; whether through dreams or vision, through prophecy or His written word — write them down. It is also beneficial to get God-given strategies for your life as regards to where you are going. The problem is that many times people are too busy crying or falling down when they are being ministered to in prayers and the prophetic (not that there is anything wrong with these when divinely inspired), however they sometimes fail to hear the fullness of what is being prophesied over them which can bring direction.

Even if you do not know where your life is going, you can ask God for a vision for your life, and even if you feel that He hasn't shown you or told you yet, know that your end is greater than your beginning as you surrender to Him and allow His hand to steer your life. Check the scriptures for God's promises concerning you. No matter what you do, have a picture of great things ahead of you — do not allow the devil distract you. Even in the midst of trials be of good cheer as John 16:33 says, knowing that there is hope for you.

You cannot fold your arms and play dead at every disappointment or set back in life, the devil isn't just going to sit back and allow you to possess your possession without a fight, he is on a mission to steal, kill or destroy, do not let him; there is more going for you than there is against you. Thank God for the promise in His word in Romans 8:31-34 that says, *"What then shall we say to these things? If God is for us, who can be against us? He who did not spare His own Son, but delivered Him up for us all, how shall He not with Him also freely give us all things? Who shall bring a charge against God's elect? It is God who justifies. Who is he who condemns? It is Christ who died, and furthermore is also risen, who is even at the right hand of God, who also makes intercession for us."*

1 John 4:4 says that, *"...He who is in you is greater than He who is in the world."* God is on your side, remember this, so press on and keep doing what you know to do, in due time He will lift you up.

PRAY:

Lord help me to redeem the time and regain any loss ground in life.

Lord, I receive power today from on high to press on, possess my possessions and to be victorious in all that comes my way in Jesus' name.

Habakkuk 2:1-4
2 Corinthians 10

40

YOU'VE BEEN SET FREE

"And you shall know the truth, and the truth shall make you free."
(John 8:32)

This verse of scripture is so critical to us as believers, because the devil holds us in bondage to things that we have been delivered from. Jesus Christ has already paid for our deliverance and He said, *"it is finished"* (John 19:30). He gave us (His disciples) the keys to the Kingdom of Heaven that whatsoever we forbid on earth is forbidden and whatsoever we allow on earth is allowed, in alignment with what has already been forbidden or allowed in heaven (Matthew 16:19). The problem is that somehow the devil afflicts us with what Jesus Christ has already delivered us from by the divine exchange on the Cross. He accuses us, confuses us, oppresses us, he tries to subdue us, but we need to stand our ground and resist him in faith with the word of God.

The preceding verse to John 8:32 *"And you shall know the truth and the truth shall make you free."* John 8:31 says, *"Then Jesus said to those Jews who believed Him, "If you abide in My word, you are My disciples indeed." (John 8:31)* "Abiding" is not merely a casual reading of the word, but a dwelling in;

hearing the word, studying the word, believing the word, meditating on the word, confessing the word and doing the word — as we do this, the word of God begins to shape us and empower us. The Bible says in Hebrews 4:12 *"For the word of God is living and powerful, and sharper than any two-edged sword, piercing even to the division of soul and spirit, and of joints and marrow, and is a discerner of the thoughts and intents of the heart."*

There is also the spoken word, where the Lord tells you situations specific to you — divine revelation. The word of God will cut through every deception and cause the truth of the word to come alive in us and bring us into glorious freedom. Even though the Lord has given us the keys to fight and overcome the enemy with in His word, we need to constantly remember that it is by His mercies that we are not consumed and not take Him for granted. I end with these words of our Lord Jesus in John 15:4 *"Abide in Me, and I in you. As the branch cannot bear fruit of itself, unless it abides in the vine, neither can you, unless you abide in Me."*

PRAY:

Lord help me to abide in You and let Your word abide in me.

Open my eyes to any area of my life that the devil is hindering and help me to know what to do about it.

Psalm 18
Colossians 2

41

DON'T DESPISE WHAT YOU HAVE

"Then they despised the pleasant land; they did not believe His word, but complained in their tents, and did not heed the voice of the LORD."
(Psalm 106:24-25)

What has God given you that you are despising? The children of Israel saw the awesomeness of God and the mighty works He did in their midst and for them; how He delivered them with a mighty hand from bondage in Egypt, the parting of the Red Sea, manna from heaven, water from the rock, His Presence that went before them in the pillar of cloud by day and pillar of fire by night, and many other signs and wonders, yet they persistently doubted Him and murmured against Him. Maybe they expected a better land or an easier land to conquer?

Don't we sometimes do the same thing? How often do we despise the days of humble beginnings? How often do we look at what others have, and get frustrated and grumble and complain, because we haven't received ours. How about when we forget the great things He has done for us, especially when we are waiting for other things to manifest. We need to be grateful for what we have, no matter how little it may seem; it is good to thank God for His mercy and His loving kindness.

When God would afflict the children of Israel for their rebellion, the Bible records that: *"Nevertheless He regarded their affliction, when He heard their cry; and for their sake He remembered His covenant, and relented according to the multitude of His mercies"* (Psalm 106:44-45). — what a good, kind Father we have. Per chance you have been complaining or despising what the Lord has given you or not given you or where He has placed you or not placed you, or the things that He is doing in your life or not doing in your life; repent and turn to Him that you may obtain mercy. He says in His word that if you are faithful with what He has given you, He will give you more (Matthew 25:21). The word of God also says that we should give Him thanks in all things, because this is His will (1 Thessalonians 5:18).

I'll end this note with this scripture from Malachi 3:13-16. *"Your words have been harsh against Me," Says the LORD, "yet you say, 'What have we spoken against You?' You have said, 'It is useless to serve God; What profit is it that we have kept His ordinance, And that we have walked as mourners Before the LORD of hosts? So now we call the proud blessed, For those who do wickedness are raised up; They even tempt God and go free.' " Then those who feared the LORD spoke to one another, And the LORD listened and heard them; So a book of remembrance was written before Him for those who fear the LORD and who meditate on His name."*

PRAY:

I give you thanks Lord for all You are to me and all You have done for me. I truly appreciate You.

Cause me to hear Your lovingkindness in the morning, for in You do I trust; cause me to know the way in which I should walk, for I lift up my soul to You (Psalm 143:8)

Numbers 11
Psalm 107

42

YOU DON'T LOVE ME

"But also for this very reason, giving all diligence, add to your faith virtue, to virtue knowledge, to knowledge self-control, to self-control perseverance, to perseverance godliness, to godliness brotherly kindness, and to brotherly kindness love. For if these things are yours and abound, you will be neither barren nor unfruitful in the knowledge of our Lord Jesus Christ."
(2 Peter 1:5-8)

One night many years back at about two in the early hours of the morning, my first son (two months short of his ninth birthday) slipped a note into my bedroom to say that he felt unloved; the note actually said, "You don't love me". That got me out of bed quickly! Thank God that he was able to communicate his feelings to me, some other child might have held it in and later on it could lead to feelings of rejection. My other two children who are younger tended to monopolise my attention, and I guess I imagined that he being older than them would understand.

This event made me realise that while doting on the others because they needed it, I must also show him more open affection. I reassured him that I loved him, and by the grace of God, I had to get the others to give me the chance to have quality time with him also. My husband and I tended to give him more "goodies" or at least more expensive goodies than the others because he's older and maybe as compensation, but gifts cannot take the place of quality time spent with your loved ones.

When I began to take time to show him and not just tell him that I loved him, he really blossomed and has become quite a confident young man. There are times though that children use the "you don't love me" speech as a weapon, when they are really saying, "you won't let me have my naughty way," however we must do what we can to show them and those around us that we love them.

The Lord has really used this to make me a better person, because I now try to take time as best as I can to let those around me know that they are special to me and I love and appreciate them. Love is not passive — it is active. Look around you, are there people that need to know that you love them? Maybe a spouse, a child, a sibling, a friend that needs that affirmation. Sow some love today and by God's grace you'll reap some too.

PRAY:

Lord let mercy, peace and love be multiplied to me. (Jude 1:2)

Grant me the grace that I need to love as I ought to and help me recognise people around me that need to experience Your love through me.

1 Corinthians 13
1 John 4

43

MY OWN STRENGTH

"He will guard the feet of His saints, But the wicked shall be silent in darkness. "For by strength no man shall prevail."
(I Samuel 2:9)

I have come to the realisation (yet again!) that I can never be who God wants me to be in my own human effort; I have tried and tried and tried again in my own strength, because I so want to be perfect and I keep falling short. It is liberating to know that it is the blood of Jesus that qualifies me and not my own human endeavours, for it is His grace working in me that empowers me to be who He has called me to be. It is essential that we seek to do right and crucial that we live right, however we must realise that our righteousness comes from the completed works of Christ on the Cross, *"not of works, lest anyone should boast"* (Ephesians 2:9).

We must not take this grace for granted though because even though salvation is free to us, it cost God something more precious than gold or silver, more precious than diamonds or platinum or any other precious jewel, or anything for that matter. It cost God His only begotten Son, Jesus Christ who suffered and died for our sins and was raised up for our justification. Titus 2:11-12 NLT says, *"For the grace of God has been revealed, bringing salvation to all people. And we are instructed to turn from godless living and sinful pleasures. We should live in this evil world with wisdom, righteousness, and devotion to God,"*

When I try so hard in my own strength to be what He has called me to be, rather than ask the Holy Spirit to help me become what I was created to be, I get frustrated. The Holy Spirit, the Helper, the Spirit of truth that proceeds from the Father is in us to help us to be what we ought to be, He gives us divine abilities to succeed, working in us both to will and to do His good pleasure (Philippians 2:13). We need to be constantly aware of the fact that we are not alone and that we are not powerless. Romans 8:14 says, *"For as many as are led by the Spirit of God, these are sons of God."* I don't want to be led by my own emotions or my own desires, I willingly submit to God and yield to the Holy Spirit so that He can stir my heart (my emotions and desires) aright.

I have had to lay down my selfish ambitions and seek after the Lord's will for my life. I may not know what to do or how to do it, but what I can do, I'll do — and that is pray. I believe that as I pray, the Holy Spirit will work on my heart to give me divine inspiration and strength for what I ought to do. So instead of just waiting for the "big break", by His grace I'll do the little that I know to do now. As I am faithful in the little things, then God is able to commit more into my hands. He is a just and merciful God.

PRAY:

Lord use me as an instrument in Your hands to accomplish Your purpose on earth.

Teach me to do Your will, for You are my God; Your Spirit is good. Lead me in the land of uprightness. (Psalm 143:10)

John 1:1-18
Philippians 4

44

DON'T LOSE HEART

"Therefore we do not lose heart. Even though our outward man is perishing, yet the inward man is being renewed day by day. For our light affliction, which is but for a moment, is working for us a far more exceeding and eternal weight of glory, while we do not look at the things which are seen, but at the things which are not seen. For the things which are seen are temporary, but the things which are not seen are eternal."
(2 Corinthians 4:16-18)

There is something about the above scripture and these verses of scripture in Hebrews 4:15-16 that come together nicely — *"For we do not have a High Priest who cannot sympathize with our weaknesses, but was in all points tempted as we are, yet without sin. Let us therefore come boldly to the throne of grace, that we may obtain mercy and find grace to help in time of need."*

In other words, no matter what you go through or are going through, Jesus cares; and somehow if you do not lose heart, but come to His throne of grace, it will work out for your good. He understands our weaknesses because He Himself came as man. If however you feel overwhelmed, ask the Holy Spirit for help and take instruction and solace from

Philippians 4:6-7 (NLT) which says, *"Don't worry about anything; instead, pray about everything. Tell God what you need, and thank him for all he has done. Then you will experience God's peace, which exceeds anything we can understand. His peace will guard your hearts and minds as you live in Christ Jesus."*

When we are standing in faith for something or the other, there are times that our faith will be tested; and mine has been several times. In these times I have done the only thing I know to do to keep from drowning in the troubles, and that is to fall into the Lord's gentle and loving arms in the place of praise, worship and prayer and allowing His presence to calm me. I then begin to encourage myself in the Lord as the Psalmist did in Psalm 42 —This is how I'm able to stand.

Many times before things get better, they look as though they are actually getting worse. Take the case of Shadrach, Meschach and Abednego in Daniel chapter three — they didn't have to be thrown into the fire before God saved them. He could have saved them before they were thrown in, but God chose to save them in the midst of the fire. The testimony was bigger that way and brought glory to God, also their reward greater, for there was no doubt that it was the hand of God that saved them.

God says in Isaiah 43:2: *"When you pass through the waters, I will be with you; and when you pass through the rivers, they will not sweep over you. When you walk through the fire, you will not be burned; the flames will not set you ablaze."* (NIV)

PRAY:

(Whatever you are going through right now, do what the

Scriptures say to do in Philippians 4:6 — Pour out your heart to Him, bring your request before Him and thank Him for everything.)

Almighty God I ask that according to the riches of Your glory, that You will strengthen me by Your Spirit with might in my inner man (Ephesians 3:16).

Psalm 16
Hebrews 10:19-39

45

GOD'S CREATION

"The LORD looks from heaven; He sees all the sons of men. From the place of His dwelling He looks on all the inhabitants of the earth; He fashions their hearts individually; He considers all their works."
(Psalm 33:13-15)

Imagine this — You created something for your own pleasure, you fashioned every bit of the object and what you created turns around and rejects you. You not only created it but you created everything around it. It then decides that, "You know what, I'll rather live my life how I want to and in fact I rather give pleasure to myself and serve other masters rather than the creator; I don't like his rules." To top it up, some even deny that they were created by you. They search for all possible ways to mimic your creation, so they can take you out of the picture so they are not accountable to you. However when things go wrong, many times they blame you and says things like "if he exists why did he let this happen?", they turn hostile and in fact other objects that you have also made, living and existing in the space you created also turn hostile with them and harden their hearts the more. Yet they never knew you, neither did they really want you, but still you get the blame? Wow!

It would hurt a lot to be rejected by what you have made, not only rejected but not acknowledged at all. Ok, maybe some do acknowledge you, but say or think, "I acknowledge you created me, but surely it's ok for me to do whatever makes me happy even if you don't like it, after all I'm not hurting anyone. Don't forget I'm doing you a favour by acknowledging you at all."

Isn't this what some of God's creation do to Him? They've suddenly grown bigger than Him and believe they don't need Him. How this must really hurt the Lord. How sad! How pitiful! How senseless! How absurd! Genesis 6:5-6 NLT says ,*"The LORD observed the extent of human wickedness on the earth, and he saw that everything they thought or imagined was consistently and totally evil. So the LORD was sorry he had ever made them and put them on the earth. It broke his heart."*

God even sent His only begotten Son, Jesus Christ into the world to save mankind, because despite the rejection, He still loves us very much and yearns for all to come to Him. Still many are still doing their on thing. *"...God's light came into the world, but people loved the darkness more than the light, for their actions were evil. All who do evil hate the light and refuse to go near it for fear their sins will be exposed. But those who do what is right come to the light so others can see that they are doing what God wants."* (John 3:19-21 NLT).

PRAY:

Lord I pray that You will enable me by Your Spirit to love you more and more.

Let my life bring praise, glory and honour to You O Lord my Father and my God.

Isaiah 40:1-11
Isaiah 55

46

GOD HAS A PLAN

Your eyes saw my substance, being yet unformed. And in Your book they all were written, the days fashioned for me, when as yet there were none of them.
(Psalm 139:16)

In Jeremiah 1:5, God said something similar to Psalm 139:16 to Jeremiah. He said, "*Before I formed you in the womb I knew you; before you were born I sanctified you; I ordained you a prophet to the nations.*" The spiritual truth that can be gotten from this is that God has a plan for your life; and if you are in His will, all things will "work together" for your good (Romans 8:28).

Put God first in all you do, and live according to His statutes and you will get all you need to be who He has called you to be. The problem is that sometimes in this life's journey we can get derailed; we can get derailed because of disobedience, sin, ignorance, rebellion and the like. Of course if you are not in Christ and living for Him, you are completely off track, if you would however come to Him or return to Him, He will redeem the time for you and orchestrate circumstances in and around your life to get you back on course.

The Lord could have taken Israel from bondage in Egypt to the Promised Land in eleven days, but they would have had to fight great battles which they were not ready for. Battles which would have caused them to fear and return to bondage in Egypt. So He took them the longer route to get the baggage of bondage off them, to prepare them and strengthen them to take their inheritance. If they had only cooperated with Him, it would not have taken them forty years. Most of the older generation died in the wilderness because of their rebellion and did not enter the Promised Land.

For some, it's not necessarily that you have done anything wrong or that you are not in the will of God as you go through trying times, but it may be part of the journey. He understands our suffering and is not unmoved by them, so we simply have to trust Him.

So many things can be said or written on this subject, but the important thing to know is that God loves you. This is His heart concerning us in Jeremiah 29:11-14 *"For I know the thoughts that I think toward you, says the LORD, thoughts of peace and not of evil, to give you a future and a hope. Then you will call upon Me and go and pray to Me, and I will listen to you. And you will seek Me and find Me, when you search for Me with all your heart. I will be found by you, says the LORD, and I will bring you back from your captivity..."*

PRAY:

Glorious Lord. I pray for the grace that I need to walk with You as I should. I surrender myself to You, perfect all that concerns me in Jesus' name.

I submit to the plan that You have for my life as written in the volumes of Your book.

Zechariah 1
Ezekiel 37

47

GOD HAS HIS WAYS

"My thoughts are nothing like your thoughts," says the Lord. "And my ways are far beyond anything you could imagine. For just as the heavens are higher than the earth, so my ways are higher than your ways and my thoughts higher than your thoughts."
(Isaiah 55:8-9 NLT)

Entering into God's rest is about submitting to God, trusting in His plan for your life and allowing Him to take charge of your life, even to the tiniest detail. This is something that happened to me many years ago and spoke volumes to me.

I had seen a dear friend's hair and I wanted to do the same thing to my hair so I booked an appointment with the hairdressers. I specifically asked for the owner of the salon to fix my hair because she did my friend's. I had plans to tell her what to do differently, but I felt to leave it in God's hands as I usually commit all my ways into His hands. Even before I cook, I always pray and ask the Holy Spirit for help.

I got to the salon on the appointed day and someone else started on my hair, a very young lady that didn't look as though she could do a good job. I was a bit upset that though I had specifically asked the owner of the salon to be the one to fix my hair she passed it on to someone else. She did a few of the braids at the back, but the young lady did everything else including the corn rows in the front.

I did not complain or make a fuss, but rather prayed that it would look good as she obviously must have been God's choice even though not my preferred choice. Pity I don't have a picture of what she did because it was absolutely beautiful and way nicer than my friend's. The single braids that the owner had done were quite loose and not to the standard of the young lady's. I felt and looked (if I do say so myself) absolutely beautiful. Thank God I allowed His choice to do it, everything I wanted she did and much more. He really does care about the little details of our lives.

There is a saying that, "every disappointment is a blessing" and in this case it truly was the case. Indeed in every disappointment if we are willing to commit it to Him and trust Him, He is able to bring a blessing out of it.

PRAY:

Lord, let a blessing come out of every disappointment in my life.

Lord You are my first love, my joy and my peace. Your thoughts towards me are good thoughts and I surrender to Your ways.

John 2
1 Kings 19:11-21

48

PRECEPTS OF LIFE FROM HEBREWS 12

"looking unto Jesus, the author and finisher of our faith, who for the joy that was set before Him endured the cross, despising the shame, and has sat down at the right hand of the throne of God."
(Hebrews 12:2)

Here are summaries of some truths from Hebrews 12 that have helped me run my race in life and I believe they will help you too.

Lay aside every weight and sin which easily ensnares you

"Do not conform any longer to the pattern of this world, but be transformed by the renewing of your mind…" (Romans 12:2 NIV). Sin gives the enemy access to your life and keeps you in bondage, so that you are hindered from running the race that God has set before you. Besides sin; past hurts, past failures, past disappointments, past traumatic events, are all weights that if not dealt with and laid down at the feet of Jesus can greatly limit you in your pursuit of destiny. Ask the Holy Spirit to help you overcome in whatever area you are struggling with, seeking help from godly counsellors or ministers if need be.

Arise and Press On

At certain times in our lives we get to "crossroads" — where we cannot explain how we feel. We may feel down and devoid of strength. At such times we feel like giving up because the enemy piles pressure on us. These are very crucial times, and our response can make or break us. More than ever before we need to fix our eyes on the Lord. We must meditate on His word, on His goodness, fellowship with other believers, rather than isolate oneself (which is the devil's strategy), except God has called you on a retreat.

The mind is the devil's battleground, so we must resist meditating on negative thoughts, so that we don't find ourselves depressed, oppressed and miserable. 2 Corinthians 10:5 says, "*Casting down arguments and every high thing that exalts itself against the knowledge of God, bringing every thought into captivity to the obedience of Christ*". If we are able to respond right, then we will breakthrough to a higher level.

Philippians 4:6-8 tells us what to do and the things to meditate on. It says, "*Be anxious for nothing, but in everything by prayer and supplication, with thanksgiving, let your requests be made known to God; and the peace of God, which surpasses all understanding, will guard your hearts and minds through Christ Jesus. Finally, brethren, whatever things are true, whatever things are noble, whatever things are just, whatever things are pure, whatever things are lovely, whatever things are of good report, if there is any virtue and if there is anything praiseworthy — meditate on these things.*"

Cut off any root of bitterness

The root of bitterness is offence and unforgiveness. It will defile you, it will hinder you — simply put, it can destroy you and others with you. Unless you are willing to let go of unforgiveness (no matter how bad the hurt) you cannot be totally free. Mark 11:25-26 says, "A*nd whenever you stand praying, if you have anything against anyone, forgive him, that your Father in heaven may also forgive you your trespasses. But if you do not forgive, neither will your Father in heaven forgive your trespasses."* If you have been badly hurt, I pray that God will comfort you, heal your heart of every hurt and grant you the grace you need to overcome and move on in life.

Do not compromise

Do not be like Esau in Genesis 25 verses 29-34 who sold his birthright for some food and the Bible says in Hebrews 12:17 that even though he wanted to inherit the blessings afterwards seeking it with tears, he was rejected. Remember, "... *Godliness with contentment is great gain"* (1 Timothy 6:6). Yes, God wants us to prosper as confirmed in 2 Corinthians 8:9 *"For you know the grace of our Lord Jesus Christ, that though He was rich, yet for your sakes He became poor, that you through His poverty might become rich."* However we are not to be consumed with riches or our quest for riches or any of our needs for that matter that we compromise.

Be thankful

Remember the case of the ten lepers in Luke 17:12-19 only one came back to thank God and he was made whole. It is only a thankful heart that gets more. *"In everything give thanks; for this is the will of God in Christ Jesus for you"* (1 Thessalonians 5:18).

PRAY:

Lord help me to run the race of life that has been planned for me with grace and endurance.

Help me to stay focussed on You.

Hebrews 12
Psalm 1

49

THE POWER OF PRAYER

"O You who hear prayer, To You all flesh will come. Iniquities prevail against me; As for our transgressions, You will provide atonement for them. Blessed is the man You choose, And cause to approach You, that he may dwell in Your courts. We shall be satisfied with the goodness of Your house, of Your holy temple."
(Psalm 65:2-4)

We are encouraged in the Bible in many ways to pray without ceasing and to pray fervently and persistently. As a Christian you can't really get by in life without prayer. Colossians 4:2 NLT says, *"Devote yourselves to prayer with an alert mind and a thankful heart."* Colossians 4:12-13 NLT also says, *"Epaphras, a member of your own fellowship and a servant of Christ Jesus, sends you his greetings. He always prays earnestly for you, asking God to make you strong and perfect, fully confident that you are following the whole will of God. I can assure you that he prays hard for you and also for the believers in Laodicea and Hierapolis."* So you see that fervent prayer is crucial.

Matthew 7:7 says, *"Ask, and it will be given to you; seek, and you will find; knock, and it will be opened to you."* This is not a "anything goes" type of statement. You can't pray for evil or sinful desires and expect to receive the answers to your prayers. Prayers that are according to the will of God are prayers with a righteous or a just cause in line with His word. 1 John 5:14 says, *"Now this is the confidence that we have in Him, that if we ask anything according to His will, He hears us."*

In Luke 18:1-8 Jesus tells the Disciples the following parable, *"Then He spoke a parable to them, that men always ought to pray and not lose heart, saying: "There was in a certain city a judge who did not fear God nor regard man. Now there was a widow in that city; and she came to him, saying, 'Get justice for me from my adversary.' And he would not for a while; but afterward he said within himself, 'Though I do not fear God nor regard man, yet because this widow troubles me I will avenge her, lest by her continual coming she weary me.' " Then the Lord said, "Hear what the unjust judge said. And shall God not avenge His own elect who cry out day and night to Him, though He bears long with them? I tell you that He will avenge them speedily. Nevertheless, when the Son of Man comes, will He really find faith on the earth?"* Sickness is unjust, debt is unjust, poverty is unjust, joblessness is unjust; anything happening in the world or in your life that's contrary to the will of God is unjust.

Romans 12:12 NLT says, *"Rejoice in our confident hope. Be patient in trouble, and keep on praying."* The English Standard Version (ESV) says, *"be constant in prayer"* Here are some examples of some people in the Bible and how divine intervention came because of fervent prayers:

Elijah:

The prophet Elijah prayed fervent, heartfelt, passionate prayers in response to the unrighteousness in the land, God heard and answered. James 5:16-18 says, *"Confess your trespasses to one another, and pray for one another, that you may be healed. The effective, fervent prayer of a righteous man avails much. Elijah was a man with a nature like ours, and he prayed earnestly that it would not rain; and it did not rain on the land for three years and six months. And he prayed again, and the heaven gave rain, and the earth produced its fruit."*

Elijah with the backing of heaven proclaimed a drought in 1 King 17:1, *"And Elijah the Tishbite, of the inhabitants of Gilead, said to Ahab, "As the Lord God of Israel lives, before whom I stand, there shall not be dew nor rain these years, except at my word."* — And there was a drought. In 1 Kings 18:1,41-45, God told Elijah to present himself before Ahab and He would send rain and rain came. So you see that His fervent prayers availed much.

He had the backing of heaven because he was a servant of God, called according to God's purpose and was on God's mission. In Jesus Christ we are not only God's servants, we are His children who are also called according to His purpose; therefore our fervent prayers can avail much too, because we are the righteousness of God in Christ Jesus (2 Corinthians 5:21) and because we also seek after righteousness.

Peter:

In the account in Acts 12:1-17, Peter was put in prison for spreading the gospel. While he was in prison the church prayed fervently for him and God sent an angel to rescue him. *"Now behold, an angel of the Lord stood by him, and a light shone in the prison; and he struck Peter on the side and raised him up, saying, "Arise quickly!" And his chains fell off his hands. Then the angel said to him, "Gird yourself and tie on your sandals"; and so he did. And he said to him, "Put on your garment and follow me." So he went out and followed him, and did not know that what was done by the angel was real, but thought he was seeing a vision. When they were past the first and the second guard posts, they came to the iron gate that leads to the city, which opened to them of its own accord; and they went out and went down one street, and immediately the angel departed from him. And when Peter had come to himself, he said, "Now I know for certain that the Lord has sent His angel, and has delivered me from the hand of Herod and from all the expectation of the Jewish people.""(Acts 12:7-11).* This shows the power of corporate prayers and should encourage us to pray fervently for those who are being persecuted for the sake of the gospel.

Daniel:

In Daniel 10, because of the revelation and vision that the Lord had given Daniel, he set his heart to seek the Lord and continued in prayers and fasting for 21 days. At the end of the fast an angel appeared to Him to reveal the answers to his prayers. His tenacity in prayer and fasting triggered a breakthrough in the heavenlies. The angel told him how he was delayed in getting to him because the prince of the kingdom of Persia (a spiritual strongman that reigned over the territory) and his cohorts withstood him for 21 days, till another angel, Michael came to fight alongside him.

This is what the angel told him. *"Then behold, a hand touched me and set me unsteadily on my hands and knees. So he said to me, "O Daniel, you highly regarded and greatly beloved man, understand the words that I am about to say to you and stand upright, for I have now been sent to you." And while he was saying this word to me, I stood up trembling. Then he said to me, "Do not be afraid, Daniel, for from the first day that you set your heart on understanding this and on humbling yourself before your God, your words were heard, and I have come in response to your words. But the prince of the kingdom of Persia was standing in opposition to me for twenty-one days. Then, behold, Michael, one of the chief [of the celestial] princes, came to help me, for I had been left there with the kings of Persia. Now I have come to make you understand what will happen to your people in the latter days, for the vision is in regard to the days yet to come." When he had spoken to me according to these words, I turned my face toward the ground and was speechless. (Daniel 10:10-15 AMP).* So we see that Daniel's continued prayer and fasting provoked a response.

Jehoshaphat:

In 2 Corinthians 20, the enemies of Judah ganged up together against them when Jehoshaphat was king. The Bible said a great multitude came against them so they feared. This drove Jehoshaphat to seek the face of the Lord and called a fast for the whole nation of Judah. When they sought the Lord, He gave them a prophetic word through a Levite called Jahaziel which gave them strength and encouragement. *"And he said, "Listen, all you of Judah and you inhabitants of Jerusalem, and you, King Jehoshaphat! Thus says the LORD to you: 'Do not be afraid nor dismayed because of this great multitude, for the battle is not yours, but God's. Tomorrow go down against them. They will surely come up by the Ascent of Ziz, and you will find them at the end of the brook before the Wilderness of Jeruel. You will not need to fight in this battle. Position yourselves, stand still and see the salvation of the LORD, who is with you, O Judah and Jerusalem!'*

Do not fear or be dismayed; tomorrow go out against them, for the LORD is with you." (2 Chronicles 20:15-17)

The Lord said, "Position yourself", so they did as the Lord said, but added thanksgiving, praise and worship to it. Jehoshaphat and the people showed their confidence in the Lord by thanking Him and worshipping Him in advance because they trusted His word. Many times we do the works (the positioning) and not the prayers. Or we do the prayers but not the positioning (the necessary action that is needed that God stirs our heart to do or what he tells us to do). James 2:20 says, "...faith without works is dead."

"Now when they began to sing and to praise, the LORD set ambushes against the people of Ammon, Moab, and Mount Seir, who had come against Judah; and they were defeated. For the people of Ammon and Moab stood up against the inhabitants of Mount Seir to utterly kill and destroy them. And when they had made an end of the inhabitants of Seir, they helped to destroy one another. So when Judah came to a place overlooking the wilderness, they looked toward the multitude; and there were their dead bodies, fallen on the earth. No one had escaped." (2 Chronicles 20:22-24). Jehoshapat and the people of Judah reaped the spoils of victory and returned to give God praise.

Whatever battles you face, with God on your side you will reap the spoils of victory in Jesus' name. The people of Judah returned to give God praise after the victory. May praise for God's victory in your life never cease. Don't get the victory and run off; their praise was their testimony that it was not by power, nor by might but it was by God's divine intervention. Don't be like the nine lepers in Luke 17:11-19, ten were healed but only one returned to give thanks to the Lord and was made whole.

God is a merciful God and we can see through the Scriptures that when He would punish Israel (and Judah) by letting their enemies attack them, whenever they returned to Him in repentance and prayer, He had compassion on them and delivered them from their afflictions, but the people still continually turned their backs on Him and returned to their wicked ways. God cannot be mocked. He is merciful and just, full of love and compassion, however don't take His grace and kindness for granted. Hebrews 12:28-29 says *"Therefore, since we are receiving a kingdom which cannot be shaken, let us have grace, by which we may serve God acceptably with reverence and godly fear. For our God is a consuming fire."*

In all our praying, let us remember to pray also for the things that are dear to God's heart. Let us pray that His Kingdom will come and His will be done on earth as it is in heaven. Let us pray for those in authority that they will do the will of God. Let us pray for the lost that they will know the Lord Jesus. Let us pray for the broken hearted that they will be comforted, let us pray for orphans that they will be placed in loving godly homes and for the poor that they will be well catered for, for the homeless that they will housed. Let us pray for those who are being persecuted for the sake of the Gospel that they will be victorious in Jesus' name. Let us seek the Kingdom of God first and as the Scripture says the other things that we are seeking will be added to us.

So keep asking, keep seeking, keep knocking in prayer, do not give up. May God divinely intervene on your behalf in Jesus' name. Know this though, that the most important bit of prayer is getting to know the Lord more intimately and fellowshipping with Him. God is not slack concerning His promises but He does not desire that any should perish. Even though this scripture in 2 Peter 3:9 is referring to the Lord's return, it can also be applied to the fact that there are some things that cannot be released to you till you are ready for it, for God makes all things beautiful in its time (Ecclesiastes 3:11).

    I would like to also encourage you to add the discipline of fasting to your prayers as you are able or as God leads you to, for there is great power in this sacrifice.

Prayers

"In the days of His earthly life, Jesus offered up both [specific] petitions and [urgent] supplications [for that which He needed] with fervent crying and tears to the One who was [always] able to save Him from death, and He was heard because of His reverent submission toward God [His sinlessness and His unfailing determination to do the Father's will]."
(Hebrews 5:7 AMP)

50

PRAYERS

"I tell you, you can pray for anything, and if you believe that you've received it, it will be yours. But when you are praying, first forgive anyone you are holding a grudge against, so that your Father in heaven will forgive your sins, too." (Mark 11:24-25 NLT)

These prayer guidelines have been put together to help you pray through different situations. Prayers are in bullet points (please tweak as necessary).

Prayers seeking after God

Start every prayer time with thanksgiving, praise and worship. Always seek to know more of God and just spend time basking in His Presence. You can also put on pure worship music quietly in the background (you can do this before, during or at the end of your prayers), the aim is to rest in His Presence and allow Him to fill you and also speak into your heart. Seek to get direction for your life from Him, and be attentive to hear His voice — rarely audible, but He speaks directly to our hearts, or through visions and dreams. With the latter though, you need to discern if it's from God because dreams and visions can come from the enemy too. If you are unsure seek mature godly counsel. Nothing you hear from

God will contradict the Scriptures.

Pray:
- I need You my Lord, I hunger and thirst for more of You.
- Father I want to know You more, open the eyes of my understanding so I can know You better.
- Help me to love You more.
- Fill me with Your fullness my Lord.
- Show me great and mighty things that I do not know — reveal heavenly secrets to me.
- Work eternity in my heart Lord.
- Fill me with Your peace.
- Fill me with Your love.
- Help me to tarry in Your Presence, so that I might know the fullness of joy that is found there.
- Infuse me with Your power dear Lord.
- Transform me with Your grace.
- Let my life proclaim Your majesty and Your goodness.
- Let me draw people to You my Lord.
- Teach me Your word and let it dwell in me richly in all wisdom.

I ask all these in the name of Jesus Christ.

Praying for a transformed life

"For we have heard of your faith in Christ Jesus and your love for all of God's people, which come from your confident hope of what God has reserved for you in heaven. You have had this expectation ever since you first heard the truth of the Good News. So we have not stopped praying for you since we first heard about you. We ask God to give you complete knowledge of his will and to give you

spiritual wisdom and understanding. Then the way you live will always honor and please the Lord, and your lives will produce every kind of good fruit. All the while, you will grow as you learn to know God better and better. We also pray that you will be strengthened with all his glorious power so you will have all the endurance and patience you need. May you be filled with joy, always thanking the Father. He has enabled you to share in the inheritance that belongs to his people, who live in the light. For he has rescued us from the kingdom of darkness and transferred us into the Kingdom of his dear Son, who purchased our freedom and forgave our sins." (Colossians 1:4-5, 9-14 NLT)

When it comes to walking in divine purpose, we cannot do much without the help of the Holy Spirit. Job 32:8 says, *"But there is a spirit in man, and the breath of the Almighty gives him understanding."* The New Living Translation (NLT) says, *"But there is a spirit within people, the breath of the Almighty within them, that makes them intelligent."* Therefore we must be continually yielded to the Holy Spirit so that He can inspire and transform us; He does this as we spend time in prayer, studying and meditating on the word.

Pray:
- Lord please give me divine understanding of Your truth and Your will.
- Father give me spiritual wisdom and understanding that I may know You more.
- Teach me Your ways my Lord and help me to walk with You better.
- Lord strengthen me with Your glorious power so that I can have all the endurance and patience I need to be who

You've called me to be.
- Fill me with joy dear Lord.
- Fill me more and more with Your Spirit.
- When I'm tested let me not be found wanting my Lord.
- Inspire me Lord by Your Spirit and make me intelligent.
- Lord help me to walk in the blessings that You have for me in this season of my life.
- Show me what to do Lord to enlarge my capacity to receive.
- I pray that I will not delay nor hinder my set time by not being prepared. Lord help me to prepare for the greater heights that You have for me. Help me to be ready for the assignment that You have for me to fulfil.
- Lord help me to put my life in order — I need Your help to do this Lord, I can't do it on my own (Psalm 127:1).
- Give me divine instructions for my future. What would you have me do? Make me sensitive to Your voice my Lord; awaken my ears to hear You.
- Lord give me divine enablement to do what You show me. Help me to walk in the realisation and the manifestation of what you've already done for me.

I ask all these in the name of Jesus Christ.

Praying to break hindrances

Especially for those whose parents or ancestors have been involved in the occult.

Pray:
- (Always start with thanksgiving, praise and worship as with every prayer)
- (Ask God for mercy where you have sinned or where there

is any charge speaking against you or your family, declare the word in Colossians 2:14 and plead the blood of Jesus Christ that was shed for the remission of sins. Confess that the blood of Jesus Christ, the blood of sprinkling is speaking better things concerning you — Hebrews 12:24).
- I appeal to the courts of heaven, to You O God, the righteous Judge, the merciful Judge that according to the works of Jesus Christ on the Cross of Calvary that You will intervene on my behalf. Let everything working against Your divine destiny for my life be demolished in Jesus' name.
- In anyway I am being beguiled or deceived by the enemy, open my eyes to see Lord. Let Your light shine into every dark place that might be in my life. Confound the enemy my Lord and destroy their works concerning me.
- Father whatever spell, whatever divination, whatever curse, whatever enchantment, whatever limitation or demonic influence is prevailing in my life or family let them be broken and destroyed in Jesus' name.
- Whatever covenants, whatever demonic vows, whatever promises or agreements were made by my parents or ancestors tying our lives to strange gods or altars. I renounce them, I reject them and I denounce them all in Jesus' name. I command every strongman or strongmen attached to whatever they did or the covenants, vows, promises or dedications that they made subdued and held captive under the name of my Lord Jesus Christ and His blood that has set me free. I forbid them access to my life and the lives of my descendants. I forbid their influence on anything that concerns us in Jesus' name.

- I am a child of God through Jesus Christ and I am also a bondservant of our Lord Jesus Christ (1 Peter 2:16) who paid the price in full for our redemption.
- Therefore I've been marked with the mark of the Lord which supersedes every other mark or incisions on my body (for those with incisions). I belong wholly to Jesus Christ and I dedicate myself and my descendants wholly to Him in an everlasting covenant ratified by blood, His blood.
- Let the effect of every negative pronouncement against our lives cease from today. Let there be restoration of the years that have been consumed or wasted, let there be restoration of the things that have been hindered.
- Lord Jesus You said that in Your name we will drive out demons (Mark 16:17), You also said in Matthew 10:1 that You have given us authority over unclean spirits to drive them out.
- Therefore as a believer and a disciple of the Lord Jesus Christ, I take the authority that I've been given and I bind and drive out all demons and familiar spirits that have been sent to harass, oppress, suppress or hinder me or my family in any way I declare all evil influences or forces coming against our lives subdued and utterly destroyed.
- I bring my life and the lives of my descendants solely and wholly under the influence of the Kingdom of God.
- (Thank God for answered prayers.)

I ask and declare all these in the name of Jesus Christ.

Praying for protection

"Therefore take up the whole armor of God, that you may be able to withstand in the evil day, and having done all, to stand." (Ephesians 6:13)

Pray:
- Lord I ask for protection. I pray for divine health, peace and security. Let Your hand be upon me to keep me from evil and to keep evil away from me.
- Lord direct my steps by Your word, let no iniquity have dominion over me (Psalm 119:133).
- Let Your angels take charge concerning me Lord to keep me in all my ways, and let Your goodness and mercy abide with me all the days of my life (Psalms 91:11 & 23:6).
- Thank You Lord for coming to destroy the works of the devil.
- Thank You Lord that no weapon formed against me shall prosper and I condemn every tongue that rises against me in judgement because this is my heritage as Your servant for my righteousness comes from You (Isaiah 54:17).

I ask all these in the name of Jesus Christ.

Praying for a miracle

"But you have come to Mount Zion and to the city of the living God, the heavenly Jerusalem, to an innumerable company of angels, to the general assembly and church of the firstborn who are registered in heaven, to God the Judge of all, to the spirits of just men made perfect, to Jesus the Mediator of the new covenant, and to the blood of sprinkling that speaks better things than that of Abel."(Hebrews 12:22-24)

Pray:
- Lord I need a miracle — please work a miracle in my life.
- Lord I want to be ready to receive my miracle; Lord help me to be ready. (Ask God to show you things that could

hinder: unconfessed sins, fear, doubt, unbelief, lack of faith, immaturity, laziness.)
- Lord whatever charge is against me, I plead the blood of Jesus Christ. (Confess your sins and ask for forgiveness. Release anyone who you have unforgiveness in your heart towards. If this is hard for you to do, ask the Holy Spirit to help you out. It starts with having a heart that's willing to do whatever the Lord requires of you.)
- Lord I release myself to You. Do Your work in me.
- Lord let my miracle be released now.
- I receive my miracle by faith in Jesus' name.
- Thank You for my miracle Lord. I believe that You have heard me and that I will see the manifestation of what You have done for me.

I ask all these in the name of Jesus Christ.

Prayers for ministry

"That is why the Scriptures say, "When he ascended to the heights, he led a crowd of captives and gave gifts to his people." (Ephesians 4:8 NLT)

Pray:
- Thank You Lord for the ministry that You have created me to fulfil. I thank You for the gift or gifts You have resourced me with for this and for the power of the Holy Spirit working in me to bring it to pass.
- Lord whatsoever is contending with this ministry, I command them pulled down and destroyed.
- Lord, let every negative pronouncement, every negative effect, every negative perception or conception the enemy

has placed on this ministry be neutralised by the power in Jesus' name.
- Father cause those You have given me to receive my ministry and let those helpers that You have assigned to help see the ministry established and fruitful be released and gathered to me.
- Lord I ask for and receive boldness to function in ministry.
- Lord let Your glory, favour, grace, presence and power and indisputable miracles be evident in the ministry You've called me to fulfil.

I ask all these in the name of Jesus Christ.

Praying for the month

The Bible says in Matthew 16:19 AMP *"I will give you the keys of the kingdom of heaven; and whatever you bind (declare to be improper and unlawful) on earth must be what is already bound in heaven; and whatever you loose (declare lawful) on earth must be what is already loosed in heaven."* Therefore prophesy into the month, for yourself, your family, your local church and even your city and nation.

Pray:
- Lord, I prophesy into this month by the power in the name of my Lord Jesus Christ,
- That I will walk in dominion power.
- That the month will bring me joy and peace.
- That this month will bring me increase.
- That I will walk in divine purpose.
- That I will have skilful godly wisdom to be and to do all You want me to be and to do.

- That I will bear good fruit in Your kingdom.
- That I will have the strength, the grace and the mercy that I need to overcome all challenges that come my way.
- That I will walk in divine health.
- That the angels of the Lord will watch over me to keep me in all my ways.
- That every person, institution or nation carrying every good You have apportioned to me this month will find me in Jesus' name.
- That I will be a blessing.
- That I will not lack for any good thing I need to fulfil purpose.
- Lord make me both a symbol and a source of blessing (Zechariah 8:13 NLT).
- I pray that every blessing and every assignment that You have for me will be fulfilled in Jesus' name.
- I pray that You will visit my life and home in a powerful way in this month.
- The Bible says in Ephesians 1:3 that You, the Father of our Lord Jesus Christ, have blessed us with every spiritual blessing in the heavenly realms because we are united with Christ. (Pray in tongues as inspired by the Holy Spirit for a few minutes if you can.) By faith I loose every blessing that are meant for me in this season of my life here on earth. The gifts that I must operate in, the jobs, creative abilities, witty inventions…Let Your Kingdom come and let Your will be done on earth as it is in heaven.
- I praise You Lord, therefore according to Your word in Psalm 67:6, let the earth yield its increase to me. I ask You to bless me Lord, because You are my God, my dear heavenly Father.

- (For those that have children, or even if you don't have any yet, pray for your nieces, nephews or those you have charge over.) I pray Your protection over my children Lord. I pray that they will not fall by the wayside, that You will preserve their lives and their destinies.

I ask all these in the name of Jesus Christ.

Praying for your spouse

(For those that are not yet married, you can still pray for the spouse that is on the way). *"The man who finds a wife finds a treasure, and he receives favor from the Lord."* (Proverbs 18:22 NLT). If you are a man pray for your wife, and a woman pray for your husband.

Pray:
- Dear Lord God, bless and keep my husband/wife. I pray for wisdom for him/her.
- I pray that he/she will be a man/woman of valour and virtue, a man/woman after Your own heart.
- I pray that he/she will love me as he/she ought to and I will do likewise too.
- I pray that we will submit to one another in accordance with Your word.
- I pray that You will make every crooked path straight for him/her and order his/her steps.
- I pray that he/she will prosper in his/her calling and his/her destiny will not be cut short.
- I pray for good health and strength for him/her.
- Let every assignment of Satan and his cohorts against my

husband/wife fail completely.
- Lord, let every demonic influence over his/her life be utterly destroyed.

I ask all these in the name of Jesus Christ.

Praying for the nations and others

"Then He taught, saying to them, "Is it not written, 'My house shall be called a house of prayer for all nations'? But you have made it a 'den of thieves.' " (Mark 11:17).

Pray:
(Can be tweaked and used for corporate prayers)
- Lord I petition You today that You will hear my prayers and answer me in Jesus' name.
- Lord let Your Kingdom come and let Your will be done on earth as it is in heaven. I align myself to Your will today. Work in me both to will and to do what pleases You.
- First I ask You for mercy for myself, for my family, for the church, even for the nation. I repent Lord and ask that You will forgive us and cleanse us of all unrighteousness.
- You said in 2 Chronicles 7:14 *"if My people who are called by My name will humble themselves, and pray and seek My face, and turn from their wicked ways, then I will hear from heaven, and will forgive their sin and heal their land."* I humble myself before You dear Lord, have mercy on us. Forgive us for when we have turned our eyes away from the suffering in the world, forgive us for when we have put our needs above Your word and will, forgive us for when we have murmured and complained. Forgive us for when we have

murmured against all God given authority rather than pray, forgive us for when we have cursed rather than blessed. Forgive the murders, the killings on our street, the killing of unborn babies. Forgive us for idolatry, for adultery, for pornography, for fornication, for all kinds of sexual perversion. Forgive us for not seeking the increase of your kingdom. Lord we are sorry. In judgement, Lord please remember mercy.
- Lord, please heal Your church, save us from seducing spirits and erroneous doctrines. Help us to uphold Your word and not compromise the truth in Your word. Sweep through Your church Lord and cleanse us from all unrighteousness.
- Lord I petition You today to heal the nations of the world and save Your people who You have called by Your name.
- I pray for our brothers and sisters in Christ all over the world who are being persecuted for their faith that You will arise on their behalf and defeat the enemy.
- I pray for the advancement of Your Kingdom in the nations. I pray for those spreading the gospel that doors of effective ministry will be opened to them and also to me too so that You may be glorified.
- Lord I pray that You will raise up leaders after Your own heart for the nations. Leaders that will restore divine order and righteousness as Your word says, *"Godliness makes a nation great, but sin is a disgrace to any people." (Proverbs 14:34 NLT)*
- Lord I cry out to You "Arise, let Your light shine upon the nations and let Your glory be seen."
- I cry out for our children, for the youth — that You will open the eyes of their understanding. I pray that they will

not succumb to ungodly worldly system, but be transformed in their thinking in alignment with Your will.
- I cry out for this nation, no more killings on our streets. Particularly I pray for the youth who are causing trouble, or who are troubled; I pray that You will stop them and captivate them with Your peace and love and heal their hearts and help them to see that there is a better future for them. Put the fragmented pieces of their lives back together and cause them to find You. Lord please intervene.
- I pray for the children that are being abused that You will defend and rescue them.

I ask all these in the name of Jesus Christ.

Praying in pursuit of purpose

Many of the hindrances we face in the pursuit of purpose and moving to a higher level in life is many times due to our thinking. The Bible speaks of our renewing our mind: that is allowing our will, our thoughts and our actions to align with His will. Romans 12:2 says, *"And do not be conformed to this world, but be transformed by the renewing of your mind, that you may prove what is that good and acceptable and perfect will of God."*

Pray:
- Lord the Bible tells us in Hebrews 4:16 that we should come boldly to the throne of our gracious God. There we will receive His mercy, and we will find grace to help us when we need it most.
- I have come today Lord, answer me according to Your word because I have come based on the completed works of Jesus

Christ my Lord and Saviour.
- Lord I humble myself before You today with a repentant heart. I acknowledge that my whole family and I have sinned and transgressed against Your word. I plead the blood of Jesus and ask that You will please forgive us our trespasses and cleanse us from all our sins and iniquities, and according to Your word restore our land — our lives, our household and family in Jesus' name.
- Cleanse me from secret faults, keep me away from presumptuous sins, let them not have dominion over me. Let the words of my mouth and the meditation of my heart be acceptable to You. (Psalm 19:12-14)
- I submit my personality to You Holy Spirit, I submit my will to You, I submit my thoughts to You. Lord, change my perception. Give me the right perspective, influence my reasoning Lord — let me reason right. I surrender to You Lord, let my will align with Your will and let my actions reflect this in Jesus' name.
- Lord I cast down every imagination, and every high thing that exalts itself against Your knowledge in my life, and I bring into captivity every thought to the obedience of Christ (2 Corinthians 10:5).
- Lord come and reign in me, fill me continually with Your Spirit till Christ be formed in me. I surrender to You, have Your way in my life.
- Help me to come into the fullness of who You have made me to be (Psalm 139:13-16). I hand over control of my life to You Holy Spirit, work in me to will and to do what pleases You (Philippians 2:13). Take me from where I am to where You want me to be and establish me in the path of destiny.

- Lord please show me things in my life that are an offence to You and help me to make them right
- Lord reveal every deception in my life.
- What adjustments do I have to make?
- (Ask for inner healing; healing of broken dreams, healing of disappointments, unfulfilled promises, healing of the emotions, rejection and whatever else you need healing for.)
- Lord give me a plan for my life and the strategies I need to implement it/them.
- It is written in Psalm 32:8 that You will guide me along the best path for my life. You will advise me and watch over me. Lord I submit myself totally to be led by the Holy Spirit and Your word. Be involved in every aspect of my life Lord.
- (Pour out your heart before God and make your request known to him, according to His word in Psalm 62:8 which says *"Trust in Him at all times, you people; Pour out your heart before Him; God is a refuge for us."*)

I ask all these in the name of Jesus Christ.

Praying against the works of the enemy

"Therefore submit to God. Resist the devil and he will flee from you." (James 4:7)

Pray:
- Our Father, Your word says in Matthew 16:19 that whatever we bind (forbid) on earth it is bound (forbidden) in heaven. Therefore Lord let whatever strongman that is in my life, or working against me or my family be bound in Jesus' name. Your word tells us that as we mention the name of Jesus every knee shall bow. Therefore I command every

strongman to bow and be gone from my life and my family in Jesus' name, because we belong to the One that is stronger than any strongman — Jesus Christ our Lord and Saviour.
- In Matthew 15:13 Jesus said, "*Every plant which My heavenly Father has not planted will be uprooted.*" Lord I pray and declare that everything that You have not planted in my life, in my family be uprooted in Jesus' name. Lord deliver me/us from any thing that defiles and uproot every defilement and every infection in Jesus' name. Clear away demonic obstacles along my/our path to progress in Jesus' name.
- It is also written in Matthew 16:19 that whatever we loose (allow) on earth is loosed (allowed) in heaven therefore according to Your word O Lord, I release all that belongs to me and my family that has been withheld by the enemy in Jesus' name.
- Lord, I declare that my/our victory is permanent because Jesus Christ has paid in full and I refuse for either myself or my family to be reinfected or setback in Jesus' name. 1 John 3:8 says, "*...For this purpose the Son of God was manifested, that He might destroy the works of the devil.*"

I pray and declare all these in the name of Jesus Christ.

Praying against witchcraft

"*For the LORD, your Redeemer, and He who formed you from the womb says this, "I am the LORD, Maker of all things, who alone stretches out the heavens, who spreads out the earth by Myself, frustrating the signs and confounding the omens of boasters (false prophets), making fools out of fortune-tellers, counteracting the wise and making their knowledge ridiculous,*" (Isaiah 44:24-25 AMP).

Pray:
- I thank You Lord that Jesus Christ has paid the ultimate price for me and that His blood is speaking better things concerning me. I repent and ask for mercy Lord were I've sinned against You and given the enemy an opening to attack me in anyway, I plead the blood of Jesus Christ. Open my eyes Lord to anything that I do or that's in my life or home that empowers the enemy, and with You helping me, I purpose to put right what you show or tell me in Jesus' name
- Lord, let every witchcraft suppressing my destiny fail and be utterly destroyed.
- Let every witchcraft agent or demonic entity coming against me not prevail against me in Jesus' name. In any way they have prevailed against me in the past, I declare their power broken off of my life and affairs.
- Lord I declare that You are with me as a mighty, awesome One, therefore my persecutors will stumble, and will not prevail against me. (Jeremiah 20:11)
- As Isaiah 8:10 says, so I declare *"Take counsel together, but it will come to nothing; Speak the word, but it will not stand, For God is with us."* Therefore I declare that no weapon formed against me shall prosper and every tongue that rises against me in judgement I condemn for this is my heritage as a servant of God for my righteousness comes from You Lord (Isaiah 54:17).

I pray and declare all these in the name of Jesus Christ.

Praying for wholeness

Everything that you are going through right now that is in

the will of God for your life, that is meant to show forth God's glory through your life or meant to work something of eternal value, ask God for the grace to go through. Paul had something in his life that was like a thorn in the flesh that he wanted God to get rid off, but the Lord didn't. 2 Corinthians 12:7-10 says, *"And lest I should be exalted above measure by the abundance of the revelations, a thorn in the flesh was given to me, a messenger of Satan to buffet me, lest I be exalted above measure. Concerning this thing I pleaded with the Lord three times that it might depart from me. And He said to me, "My grace is sufficient for you, for My strength is made perfect in weakness." Therefore most gladly I will rather boast in my infirmities, that the power of Christ may rest upon me. Therefore I take pleasure in infirmities, in reproaches, in needs, in persecutions, in distresses, for Christ's sake. For when I am weak, then I am strong."*

God is more interested in our eternal destiny than in just making us "happy for the moment". He wants to work something of eternal value in us. His thoughts towards us are good thoughts and He will make all things work together for our good as we trust Him (Romans 8:28). The hardest thing for us when we are going through something is that it hurts, but when we claim and receive His grace as we remain in Him, trust Him and pray, we are able to better bear it and maybe even rejoice as we go through. However, what is not of God in our lives we should resist. The Holy Spirit is the One who teaches us to discern what is of God or what is not. So the first thing to do is to submit to God, then resist the devil.

Jesus Christ is not unmindful of our weaknesses. If He was He wouldn't have died for us. God send His only begotten Son to come in the flesh to take the punishment for our sins upon Himself —to take your death and give you His life. Yes, He loves you. He loves me. He loves us. His intention is not to withhold good from you, however He sees the bigger picture. He knows what you do not know. *"Oh, how great are God's riches and wisdom and knowledge! How impossible it is for us to understand his decisions and his ways! For who can know the LORD's thoughts? Who knows enough to give him advice? And who has given him so much that he needs to pay it back? For everything comes from him and exists by his power and is intended for his glory. All glory to him forever! Amen."* (Romans 11:33-36 NLT).

It is in doing what you were created for that you find rich fulfilment. As believers when our sojourn here on this earth ends, we will stand before the judgment seat of Christ, not to be sent to hell if of course we remain in Him, but to account for what we did while here on earth. We may not be judged according to all the fabulous works we did but by whether we fulfilled what He called each one of us to do and we will receive a reward for this, because you can do seemingly great things for God according to your own desire but leave what He has told you to do or called you to do undone. *"Therefore we make it our aim, whether present or absent, to be well pleasing to Him. For we must all appear before the judgment seat of Christ, that each one may receive the things done in the body, according to what he has done, whether good or bad."* (2 Corinthians 5:9-10).

Pray:
(Start with thanksgiving. The Bible says in I Thessalonians 5:16-18 *"Rejoice always, pray without ceasing, in everything give thanks; for this is the will of God in Christ Jesus for you."*)
• Lord I ask for the grace that I need at this time of my life —

help me to live the life of an overcomer.
- Lord as You have written concerning me so let it be in Jesus' name (Acts 17:26-28).
- Work in me to will and to do Your good pleasure. I yield my will to You, I yield my emotions, I yield my mind, I yield my body, I surrender my spirit to You, I surrender all to You. Have Your way in me my Lord.
- Whatever sin (known or unknown) has laid sway over my life, Lord please have mercy on me in Jesus' name. I plead the blood of Jesus that has made atonement for my sins — past, present and future and I receive forgiveness of sins and cleansing from all impurities in Jesus' name.
- *"Search me, O God, and know my heart; test me and know my anxious thoughts. Point out anything in me that offends you, and lead me along the path of everlasting life." (Psalm 139:23-24 NLT)*
- Thank You Lord for breaking down every barrier that has stood in the way of my advancement in life in Jesus' name; whether spirituality, emotionally, financially, physically — in every way.
- Thank You Lord that I will not pray amiss, but through faith in the name of Jesus Christ I command every mountain of defeat in my life to move out of my way. Everything that has stood in the path of my progress in life I command to move out of my way in Jesus' name. Whatever empowers these mountains I command to be pulled down. Whether it be wrong thoughts, wrong emotions, wrong actions, things in my lineage, I command everything to come into alignment with Your perfect will. (1 John 5:4)
- Lord let every stronghold in my life be demolished in Jesus'

name. Every imagination and high thing that exalts itself against Your knowledge in my life I pull down. Help me to see right O Lord, help me to think right, help me to say right, help me to do right. Lord I thank You that I'm Your child, so I have the mind of Christ. Thank You Lord that I have eternal life.
- Everything that is not of You in my life I command to be broken off of me this instant by the power in the name of Jesus. Let every demonic entanglement or influence over my life be destroyed right now in Jesus' name.
- Thank You Lord for breaking every limitation off of me:
  - Break off every limitation from my upbringing.
  - Break off every limitation from wrong perception.
  - Break off every limitation from the way people see me.
  - Break off every limitation from my lineage.
  - I renounce every foreign god in my life and/or in my lineage.
  - Break off every limitation brought on by fear in my life. (For You have not giving me the spirit of fear (2 Timothy 1:7).
- Thank You Lord Jesus for You have paid the price for my total salvation. You have freed me from the power of curses and I claim this freedom. I am blessed and no one can reverse it. Let every curse operating in my life be broken because this is unjust because Jesus has paid in full. Therefore let there be a reversal of every limitation this might have brought upon my life. I receive deliverance. I receive wholeness. I receive my healing. I receive complete liberty. I claim the victory that I have in Christ Jesus — Amen! (Galatians 3:13-14)

- I am yoked to Jesus Christ, so I cannot be anyone else's slave. I belong to Jesus. Therefore whatever has either enslaved or is trying to enslave me is usurping authority, so I command them to bow to Jesus and be gone.
- Lord let everything that is not of You in my life fall of me right now in Jesus' name. Help me identify the things that I need to deal with my Lord. (Perhaps things in my home that gives the enemy access to me that I need to get rid off —Exodus 20:4-5).
- Every demonic entity sent to watch my life to frustrate me, I command to be held captive under the name of our Lord Jesus and I cast them away from me never to return.
- Lord cause me to arise out of slumber and put on strength.
- Lord I ask for more of You in my life, let there be a mighty outpouring of Your Spirit over my life. Let the Holy Spirit fill me to overflow and come on me like a cloak in Jesus' name.
- Lord stir up in me every dormant gifting and calling and anoint me this day with the anointing I need to function in what You've called me to do.
- Lord I thank You for who I am in Christ Jesus and I agree with Your word and therefore declare and confess by faith that:
  - I am the head and not the tail, I'm on top and not at the bottom because Jesus Christ has paid the price for me in full.
  - Because of the sacrifice of the Lord Jesus I have passed out from under the curse and entered into the blessing of Abraham who You blessed in all things.
  - By the stripes of Jesus Christ I am healed.

- I am more than a conqueror
- I have an excellent spirit because Your Spirit is in me
- I will live to declare Your works in the land of the living.
- No weapon formed against me shall prosper, every tongue that rises against me in judgement I condemn in Jesus' name for this is my heritage as Your servant because my righteousness comes from You (Isa. 54:17).
- I am a child of God.
- I have the mind of Christ.
- I am abundantly blessed and rich because of the Your generous grace. The Scriptures says of Jesus that though He was rich, yet for our sakes He became poor, so that by His poverty He could make us rich (2 Corinthians 8:9). Thank You, Lord!
- I claim all the blessings of the divine exchange on the Cross.
- I am a joint heir with Christ.
- I thank You for soundness of spirit, soul and body
- From today I walk in dominion power in Jesus' name.
- Thank you Lord that I'm victorious because you have destroyed the works of the devil, so I walk in victory covered by the blood of Jesus Christ.

I ask and declare all these in the name of Jesus Christ…Amen!

I leave you with this sure way to be blessed in Psalm 41:1-3 NLT *"Oh, the joys of those who are kind to the poor! The LORD rescues them when they are in trouble. The LORD protects them and keeps them alive. He gives them prosperity in the land and rescues them from their enemies. The LORD nurses them when they are sick and restores them to health."*

Lightning Source UK Ltd.
Milton Keynes UK
UKHW02f1919020318
318785UK00006B/220/P